The Education Handbook
for
Foster Carers
and
Adopters

Anne Peake

Published in 2017 by

Russell House Publishing Ltd
The Coach House
Ware
Lyme Regis
Dorset
DT7 3RH

Tel: 01297 443948

E-Mail: jan@russellhouse.co.uk

www.russellhouse.co.uk

©Anne Peake

All rights reserved. No part of this publication may be reproduced, stored in a retrieval system or transmitted in any form, or by any means, electronic, mechanical, photocopying, recording or otherwise, without written permission of the copyright holder and the publisher, or without a license permitting copying in the UK issued by the Copyright Licensing Agency Ltd, Saffron House, 6-10 Kirkby Street, London, EC1N 8TS.

British Library Cataloguing-in-Publication Data:
A Catalogue record for this book is available from the British Library

ISBN: 978-1-905541-95-9

Dedicated to the memory of Chris Sey
Principal Educational Psychologist
and formerly a child in care

Cover design by Rowan, aged 9 years

Thanks to Liz Kelly for her skill and patience

Contents

Introduction

		Page
1.	Choosing a school for your child..	3
	Question – Adoption, settling in before school starts	8
2.	Reading to children and hearing them read at home	9
	Question – Screen times	13
3.	School matters.	16
	Question – Self esteem	25
4.	The role of the Designated Teacher	27
	Question – The work of the Virtual school.	29
5.	Personal education plans	31
	Question – PEP meetings	35
6.	Special educational needs	37
	Question – Repeating a year in school	43
7.	Supporting children in school	45
	Question – Temper outbursts	58
8.	That all important transition from primary to secondary school ..	61
	Question – School files	70
9.	Support for children doing homework	72
	Question – Behaviour problems in school.	79
10.	Managing your child's use of computers and the internet	80
	Question – Mobile phones	87
11.	Exams..	91
	Question – Exclusions	95
12.	Glossary	97

Introduction

Foster carers and adopters work miracles every day. They care for children whose lives have often been blighted by, at best, poor care, and at worst, abuse. While we hope that all moves for children are planned, many are not. The children can arrive with little notice, feeling uncertain and confused. There is always the expectation that they will attend school. We know that success in school increases life chances later on. For these very vulnerable children, success in school is not easy. They have to deal with: changing school when they move from their family, learning to trust the teachers when previously they may have not been supported in school, and trying to believe that they can be successful learners, yet all the while feeling 'different' from those around them. It is a government priority to raise their achievements in school and you, as parents/carers, have a major role in this.

'My old mum and dad locked me and Matt in a room. Then Matt decided to jump out of the window to find food. I don't remember my old mum and dad that much.

Being adopted is like a second chance in life. Me and my brother Matt were in six foster homes in six months.

I felt sad, lost, scared, when I was moving homes. When my new mum and dad adopted me I was worried, nervous and confused. When I got to know them more I got settled and more happy.

Going through what I went through is like a disease that stays and it is a stain that does not fade.

You can talk to your parents, friends, family members or teachers. Nothing worth doing is easy'.

Jess aged 14 years

Schools are complex places involving: the National Curriculum, hierarchies of staff, a variety of teaching methods, anxiety-provoking tests and examinations, support agencies, and as many opinions as there are people. This Handbook is for foster carers and adopters. The Handbook provides guidance with regard to supporting your child in school and building those all-important relationships with teachers and schools. Its aim is to provide information, ideas, answers to frequently asked questions and to explain the language used in Education and Social Care. It can be read as it is or used as a reference source when issues arise. It is enriched by the comments and insights of parents/carers and children. My thanks go to them for their contributions.

For teachers reading this, never underestimate what you can do to help this special group of children.

1. Choosing a school for your child

When you have a child placed with you, with the exception of babies and toddlers, the placement will usually mean you will be looking for a school. Schools vary; they may vary in ways which reflect the ruling body of the school, such as Faith schools or Free schools or Independent schools. They will also vary in size. There is no rule of thumb to tell you how to make a choice. You should visit the schools from which you want to select one. While you are the person choosing, do remember you are looking on behalf of your child, who will have had a disrupted early life, be facing great changes, may have special needs, and most of all, needs to feel welcome and included in every aspect of school life. What follows are suggestions of aspects of schools about which you might want to ask.

Location - All schools have a catchment area. Your address will be in the catchment area of a primary school and the secondary school to which the pupils move on. The expectation is that you will use your local school. There are advantages to this. It will be nearby, your child can go to school with local children from amongst whom they will make friends, you can get to know other parents who may be a network of friends and support to you and your family. You can choose another school, provided that school is not full and you undertake getting your child to and from the school. If you chose a different school from a local one, ask yourself if the school you want is convenient for home and safe for travel, whether on foot, by bus, or car.

The local secondary school - All primary schools are in 'partnerships' and feed into a local secondary school. Find out about the secondary school for the primary school. It is a big decision to move a child at their end of their primary school education to a secondary school, which is not local. This will mean, travelling further to school, your child moving on and away from established friendships and it may be difficult to secure a place if you have chosen a school which gets a high level of applications for places. There may be good reasons for your decision. By then you will know more about your child and her/his needs and feel sure about seeking a different provision or change of ethos or a fresh start for a child, when things have not gone well at primary school.

League tables - Read the most recent OFSTED report on the school. This will give you a snapshot in time of the school with its strengths and weaknesses. Look particularly at the targets set for the school. Remember that just because a school is judged to be outstanding, that doesn't mean it is right for your child. Do avoid selecting a school solely on the basis of the league tables. The results are an overall average of achievements. When looking at the league tables, look at the long term academic profile of the school, not just the results for one year. Is the school moving upwards or downwards? What you need for your child is a school which will include your child, promote progress and support her/him to feel a successful learner.

Check different sources for information - You can ask local parents who have children at the school. If you ask general questions, you will get general answers. Try asking specific questions such as what do you like most about the school? What do you like least about the school? What do local shopkeepers say about the school? What do parents/teachers at other schools say about the school? Has the school been in the local press?

Size of the school - A small primary school in a rural authority can have as few as 60 pupils, while a large primary school may have as many as 450-550 pupils. A small local secondary school may have 600 pupils, while a large local secondary may have over 2,000 pupils on a large school site or on split sites. You may feel the size of the school is a key factor. Size can bring with it advantages and disadvantages with regard to what might be best for your child.

Early Years provision - If your child is not yet at school, then you will be looking at Early Years provision. Many primary schools have nursery classes where the plan is that children attend on a part time basis, moving on to full time in a reception class in the school. The staff in the nursery will be working with the school staff and transitions will be jointly arranged. You may wish to choose an independent nursery or a preschool playgroup. Whatever you choose, visiting different settings is a must. When you visit you should look at the numbers of children, how children at different developmental stages are managed, staffing and in particular that each child has a key worker, the space for outside play and places/hours available. You should also ask how children are supported to cope with the full-time/transition to school.

Security of the school site - All schools need to be both secure and welcoming. When you visit a school, look at the way the space between the car park/entrance is managed with the play areas for the children. When you enter the school you should find the door to the building or beyond the entrance is a secure door. You will be asked to sign in and to wear a visitor's badge. This is necessary security for schools. If your child has already had some time in school prior to being part of your family and has experienced difficulties which have included running out of school, then you need to discuss this on your visit, with regard to the perimeter fencing of the grounds/nearby roads.

Play areas - When you visit a school, make sure you look at the school grounds and the playground. Is there space to play? Is the space well designed with safety features? Are there places for quiet/small children? Ask about the supervision at playtime? Can supervisors see all areas? It is a good idea to make sure you see a break time. Then you can judge for yourself how the children are playing/interacting. How are the adults interacting with the children?

The condition of the school and site - School buildings vary in age and condition. A brand new building doesn't make a school good, any more than an old building makes a school unsatisfactory. However, new designs for schools can make for spacious, light and flexible areas, which enhance the learning environment, and these add to the comfort of every one, adults and children. What is the condition of the fabric of the buildings? Litter? Is there graffiti? Is the furniture adequate, maintained and comfortable? Are the classrooms cramped? Look at walls, are they full of displays of children's work and looking like they have been carefully mounted and regularly refreshed? Visit the toilets, as the state of them will say a lot about the care of the school for the pupils.

Resources of the school - As well as classrooms, primary schools will have spaces for a school assembly, a computer suite, a hall/gym space for indoor PE, and some have a swimming pool or use a local leisure centre pool to teach swimming. Many schools also organise teaching cycling proficiency for pupils. If you are looking at secondary schools they will have dedicated subject areas such as: a science block, a drama department and facilities to stage productions, music rooms, a gymnasium and outdoor pitches, art rooms, rooms for teaching ICT, a library and much more. If your child is showing abilities/interests in a particular subject area, make sure you see the facilities for that subject. Check the school's specialism and the advantages this may offer for your child.

Visiting the school - Schools are very busy places. There will be a limit to the time they can give you for a visit. It will help if you make a list before your visit, of things you want to ask and see. Your tour of the school should include access to different areas, ask yourself: do the children look happy? What is the level of engagement of the pupils? Does the Head know the names of the pupils? How do pupils respond to the Head and to visitors? What does the Head say are the core values of the school?

Staffing - In the end, it is the staff who make the school. A settled staff group with a low turnover rate brings stability. Taking care how you ask! You might want to ask does the school have stable leadership? How long has the Head been in post? If the Head is a recent appointment, how long was the last Head in post? How is the support for special needs organised and delivered? What are the rates of staff turnover each year? What are the rates of staff sickness and are any staff on long-term sickness? In a large school, what is the school's use of cover/supply teachers?

Curriculum - the National Curriculum sets out the programmes of study and attainments for all four key stages. All local authority maintained schools must teach these programmes of study. The National Curriculum means all children in different schools study the same subjects to similar standards. Other types of schools, such as Academies and Independent schools do not have to follow the National Curriculum. All schools are inspected by OFSTED which makes judgements about the quality of the teaching. You may have preferences with regard to the curriculum for your child such as foreign language courses, faith based teaching, the inclusion of all faiths or none, musical opportunities to sing, play music and have specialist music tuition, sporting opportunities and the types of sports taught.

Behaviour in school - The school's behaviour policy and policy about bullying will be on the school website. When you read these, good questions to ask yourself could include. What are the rewards for good behaviour? What are the sanctions for inappropriate behaviour? Ask how many pupils have had fixed term exclusions over the last year.

Talking to pupils in the school - As you visit a school, it may be that during your tour, you get the chance to talk to pupils. This may well give you some insight into the school ethos, in terms of the way the pupils respond to you, their enthusiasm for the school, and their self confidence.

Pupil Premium - Pupil premium funding is additional funding made to publicly funded schools in England, to raise the attainment of disadvantaged pupils and close the gap between them and their peers. Schools receive £1,900 for each pupil who is in the looked after system, adopted, subject to a special guardianship order/child arrangements order or a residence order. Premiums are also made for children who are eligible for free school meals and children in service families. Schools manage this funding in different ways and report how the funding has been used, on an annual basis, to their governing body. This report may be on the school website. Certainly, you might want to ask how the school uses the funding, as your child will bring additional funding into the school. The money is not spent on individual children, it is usually used for resources and support to benefit these groups of disadvantaged children.

Mealtimes - Mealtimes are an important part of a school day. The school's healthy eating policy will be on the website. On your visit you can look out for: Is there a dining room/area? Does it cater for all the children? Is food cooked on the premises? How many children eat the school meals or bring packed lunches? How are the children seated? Can a child who eats a school meal sit by a friend who has a packed lunch?

Uniform - Schools usually have a uniform. The website will show you what this entails and the cost. At secondary school, there will be additional items to buy such as a PE kit, maybe a leotard and a science overall.

Before or after school activities - Many schools have breakfast clubs on some days a week. In addition, schools can have clubs/activities after school. You can ask about the types of clubs, the days on which these are available and the cost. For schools, which are in rural areas where the majority of the children come to school on school buses, there may be a limit to the number of after school activities available, picking up pupils after these can then fall to parents. Schools do trips/residential stays, which are enriching activities for pupils, so do ask about these. At secondary school, there is usually a charge for these. Some schools hold events/classes for people outside school.

How does the school involve parents? - Schools need to be in touch with parents and have good relationships with them. You can ask if parents can come into school to settle their child, where do parents wait at the end of the day, do teachers oversee the children as they leave the school and with whom, when will you get a school report and when is parents' evening. Ask if any parents are involved in after school clubs/activities. You might want to contribute to a club or set one up. All schools have one or more Parent Governor(s).

Choosing a school for your child is a big decision. There is no formula that can give you the answer. The majority of children do very well in their local schools, where the staff work very hard to provide a high quality education and where the pupils achieve their potential. What you need to remember is that there is so much that you can do as parents to support your child in school and to support the school. Above everything, children need to be happy in school. If they are happy, they will want to go to school, they will make friends, they will make progress in their learning, and grow as individuals in self esteem and social confidence.

Written by Anne Peake, with input from the Thursday group of parents in Britannia Road Family Centre, and ideas from Working the System - How to get the very best State Education for your child by Francis Gilbert, published by Short Books.

Adoption - Settling in before school starts

We have just been to the Adoption Panel and have been accepted as prospective adopters. We don't have children of our own and we are keen to be well prepared to help our child settle with us in the best ways possible. We feel it would be helpful to a child new to our family, to have some time with us before starting school, while we all get to know each other and we work to establish a bonding relationship with the child. At this stage we have no idea how long this might take, it could be a few days or much longer. What is the law with regard to this and how would the Local Authority and schools regard our request?

Prospective Adoptive Parents

Once you know the age of the child joining your family, you need to be thinking about registering them with either a primary or secondary school. Most parents opt for their child to attend a local school, but provided there are places available, you can chose a school, which is further away. If the child is of school age, i.e. over 4 years, then she/he will be already registered with a school and moving to live with you will, from the Local Authority point of view, entail a school transfer. Whether you are registering the child for the first time in a school or registering a transfer of school, you need to go into school and see the Head teacher. You may be wondering what surname to use when registering your child. You need to discuss this with your adoption worker.

If you feel that you want to delay the child's start at the school, while she/he settles with you, you can negotiate this with the Head teacher of the school. You will find that the Head teacher will be sympathetic. It is in everyone's interests for your child to be helped to settle into your family and to then start at a new school when you feel she/he is ready. Most children want to be like their peers and you may find your child keen to get to school.

2. Reading to children and hearing them read at home

Reading to your child is enjoyable for you both, it is an investment in your child's abilities and motivation to read, and it is a shared activity on which you both can build a close relationship. Reading to children can start as soon as they are born, with parents talking to their children, singing rhymes and showing age appropriate pictures. The benefits of reading to children include:

- The opportunity to signal to your child that she/he is your priority. You are showing that you have set aside a time when your focus is entirely on them. This builds a sense of well-being and security.
- Sharing books, if done well, teaches looking. Together you can look at the book, examine illustrations and share ideas, while you look at each other.
- Reading to children helps them to develop their vocabulary; hear language used to good effect, for example for humour or suspense, and to follow and understand narrative.
- It models for your child that you have an interest in reading. Children watch what we do and what we do provides some of the most influential teaching in their lives. It is the best basis for them learning to read.

When you read aloud to a child, you can enhance the experience for you both if you: choose an age appropriate book; read it beforehand so you are prepared; perform the dialogue and the story with voices, gestures and dramatic pauses; ask questions which engage and stimulate the child, such as 'what do you think will happen next? Is he a good pirate? What do you like about this story? When you talk about your pleasure in books and reading, you are giving your child this as a gift.

There will be times when it isn't possible for you to read to your child. These can be on a car journey, or during a long wait for an appointment, or when your child has had their bedtime stories but is taking time to settle. At such times, your child can use audiobooks and headphones to hear action rhymes, children's books and for older children set books, which are on the school curriculum.

Just as you can be involved with reading to children from a very early age, it is important to continue with reading to them, long after they have begun to learn to read for themselves. Learning to read is not a quick process especially in the early years, it will take time and patience. Children learn to read words on a page before they are able to understand what the words mean and follow a story or extract the meaning from what they have read. So continuing to read to your child is important. When an adult reads, the child can focus on the story and the characters, unhindered by their ability to read. It remains a special shared time. Even older children can enjoy being read to every day, such as a chapter of Harry Potter or a book about a special interest, having an adult read to you, particularly at bedtime can be calming while firing the imagination.

For children who have had disrupted childhoods, they may well have missed out on being read to and being heard to read. They may have come from homes where there were few or no books and no investment in the love of reading. They may have had parents who were themselves unsuccessful in school and who may not have known how best to support their children. Some of the children may have already had experiences of not doing well in school and see themselves as unsuccessful learners. Parents/carers need to be mindful of this and can help their children by promoting an interest in books and reading.

Parents/carers are often confused when their children begin to learn to read. Schools teach the sound of the letter, rather than its name. This means that when they recognise the shape of a letter on the page, it will represent a sound that they hear and which is a part of a word. Children learn to sound out letters and build these up into a word, c-a-t is cat.

Before you start to hear your child read at home, you should bear in mind the following:

- **Have books in your home which are age appropriate and which match your child's interests or stimulate their attention.** You can buy books, new and secondhand, have regular trips to your local library and if your child is of school age, borrow books from school.

- **It is best to hear a child read on a regular basis.** This gives the child the opportunity for regular practice. Hearing them read every day for a week and then not at all for a week is not helpful. If you give up or allow yourself to be regularly interrupted, you can hardly expect your child to keep on trying.

- **It is best to hear a child read for a short period of time.** Ten to fifteen minutes each day is enough. Pre-school children get very tired and if your child has been in school all day, she/he will be tired too. A short period of time also means you are less likely to see it as burdensome.

- **It is far better to end the session with the child still feeling enthusiastic than to let the child read on and on until she/he is tired.** When your child is really enjoying their time reading to you, she/he will probably want to prolong the time. When children are tired, they can quickly become short-tempered, and despite their earlier eagerness to read, they will remember sessions which ended badly and be less inclined to read in the future. When you know your child is becoming tired, you can end the session on a positive note by suggesting 'one more paragraph/page and then no more till tomorrow', followed by agreeing to look at a picture book together, or having a cuddle.

Here are some simple does and don'ts:

- **Do make sure that the atmosphere is calm and relaxed.** If the children have been squabbling and you have had to 'lay down the law' and insist on order, then it may not be the best time. If either you or your child is reluctant to read, then the session is not likely to go well.

- **Do have your child sitting very close to you in a way which you feel will help her/him to feel secure and valued.** This is a very special time, especially for children who because of circumstances beyond their control, have had experiences of loss and abandonment. You can do so much by helping your child to feel comfortable and secure in your undivided attention and love.

- **Do talk about the book first, look at the pictures, and if you are reading part of the same book each time - then remember together what has happened so far.** This gives you and your child time to settle down, get in tune with each other, and engage with the book. You can exchange views such as: wondering about the story, talking about your favourite character, or imagining what is going to happen. Your interest will stimulate your child's interest.

- **Do read a paragraph or page yourself first, to bring out the idea of the characters and story.** This can help to engage the child's interest. For very young children for whom reading is an uncertain skill, asking them to read a line or a paragraph may be enough, with you taking up the reading again to avoid overtaxing your child. New readers can have to expend so much effort sounding out the words that they lose a sense of the meaning. Taking turns to read, with the child reading just a sentence or two, makes it a joint activity, moves the story on and reduces the chance of your child getting tired or feeling defeated.

- **Do help by telling the child what the word is, when she/he gets stuck.** It is not helpful to make them try to read a word they find difficult, over and over again or to guess. Tell them the word and repeat the sentence that contains it. Explain the word so your child knows what the word and the sentence means. You can do this by using the story so far, or the pictures in the book, or your own explanations. Once she/he knows the word, you can look together at how the sounds within the word are made up. Be careful not to dwell too much on a difficult word whereby you lose sight of the story and having a relaxed time together.

- **Do make the session enjoyable and fun, by incorporating joy and praise for your child.** When your child misreads a word or gets stuck, it is best to praise their attempts with a 'good try' or 'nearly'. Signal your enjoyment of your time together with good eye contact, smiles, an interest in the book, nurturing touches and praise. Make it clear that you are enjoying the session with them.

- **Do be alert to the possibility that a session is not going well.** Try to think why that might be and if you can, rectify what you are doing to make it go better. Children are less able to modify what they do and if it is not going well because your child is tired or not enjoying the book, talk about what has gone well and bring it to an end. If both you and your child are not enjoying the time, then you should not continue.

Here are some ideas on why it may not have gone well:

- **The timing was wrong.** If it is too soon after school, they may be tired and want to relax. If the timing is just before a favourite television programme or before going out to play, the child gets a reward straight afterwards. Leaving it too late, risks your child being tired, and you may be inviting a battle.

- **There is background noise/activity, such as the television being on at the same time or an older child playing music.** No matter how good the book is, it is likely to be no match for CBeebies, Blue Peter, the Simpsons, and so on, or the whoops of a teenager playing a computer game.

- **It may be that your child feels she/he has to do better than other children.** It should never be about what other children can do. Do avoid questions about the levels of reading books of classmates. Children are best encouraged to improve on what they have done previously, and hearing a child read is about enjoyment for you both.

- **If your child doesn't want to read, don't criticise the child, ask yourself why this is the case.** Have you chosen the wrong time, the wrong book, or the wrong approach?

- **Reading is not a chore that has to be done at all costs.** Leaving it for an evening can sometimes be the most sensible decision at the time.

- **Never threaten to tell your child's teacher if she/he won't read.** If you do, they won't want to read at school either.

Remember regular, calm, interesting sessions, which you both enjoy, are likely to have the best effects.

Screen times

My son is nine years old. He has a play station, an Xbox, a tablet, and he now wants a phone. I can see that he is becoming more and more attached to his gadgets. He will frequently decline invitations to go out and play with children locally. He is spending more time in his bedroom. He says he has lots of friends online and he plays with them. I am feeling left behind in terms of what I know about these devices and I worry about the impact on him of some of the games he plays. When I suggest switching the devices off, he flatly refuses.

Adoptive Dad

Screens are a part of all our lives. Television, computers, tablets and smartphones have a range of purposes such as:

- Passive recreation - watching television, reading newspapers and books, listening to music, live streaming of plays and concerts.
- Resource for learning - fact checking, seeking opinions, sharing ideas and online learning.
- Communication - telephone calls, face-to-face calls, video chatting, social media, Instagram messaging, twitter
- Creativity - the use of devices to make digital art from sounds and images.

Screens are valuable in very many ways. It is virtually impossible not to be dependent on screens for some aspects of our lives. The issue is how parents can manage screen times with their children, alongside family life, leisure activities and the demands of school. Studies show that excessive screen time by children is linked to obesity, poor sleep, and undermining of educational progress. When children spend more time looking at screens than they do with parents, siblings and playing, this can also lead in some instances to limited social skills, a rise in aggression and behavioural difficulties.

Screen inventory. The older children are, the more time they spend looking at screens and the harder it is for them, and for you as parents, to reduce the time. If you are reading this and you have young children, this is a very good time to think about managing screen times for them. If you have older children, then you are going to need to think about your strategies for helping your children to understand how to have a balance of their screen use with other aspects of their lives. It is basic, but a good starting point is to make an inventory of the screens in your home: televisions, desktop and laptop computers, play stations, Xbox and mobile phones (include adult phones).

Audit screen usage. All children learn more from watching what we do than from listening to what we say. Try checking your own usage of screens. There are apps for phones, which can do this for you, checking each time you look at your phone and the time spent on calls and games. You can add in the times that you have the television on in rooms where you are, so don't think that the television on in the kitchen while you cook doesn't count. When you get to managing screen time with your children, you will find it harder than ever to counter their assertion that having the television on in the room where they do their homework doesn't count either. Once you have an idea about the amount of screen time, this becomes a baseline for you to measure whether you can reduce it.

Protect babies and small children. Children's brains are developing rapidly in the early years of life. There is good evidence that screen viewing by babies and small children has lasting negative effects on language development, reading skills, short term memory, and contributes to problems with sleep and attention. A parent with a toddler speaks on average 940 words an hour. With the television on, this number drops to 170 words per hour. The Royal College of Paediatricians and Child Health recommend that children under two years should not spend any time looking at television, computers and electronic games. It takes two years before a baby's brain develops to a point where symbols on a screen come to represent real life equivalents. Babies need to interact with parents/carers, siblings and other children. Their physical play contributes to their physical, mental, language, social and emotional development. After two years, pre-school children can benefit from watching educational interactive programmes alongside a familiar adult.

Take a close look at your family schedule. As parents/carers you can review what you all do as a family, if your children are old enough they can join in the discussion. Each person can use a week at a view diary and put in what they do, such as dog walking, regular clubs, out with friends, sport, with a record of the time spent on each. This will tell you what the balance is for each of you and for the family between screen times, socialising and exercise. This can lead into a discussion about encouraging more time spent socialising or exercising. Time spent at a swimming club or playing football brings social and health benefits which can't come from screen time. You can show your commitment to these benefits by giving your active support to activities which compete with screen time, by providing transport, including your child's friends, joining in some activities for example, maybe the football team need help that you can give.

Have family rules. You will have family rules about lots of things, screen times can be in your house rules. Most parents/carers find that their grasp of technology is soon overtaken by that of their children. Try to keep up, read reviews of developments/research, and use your judgement with regard to what is age appropriate for your child. An age rating on a game or film is a guide, it is up to you to decide. Explain your values and judgements to your child. If you are faced with complaints that all their friends are watching what you have decided is unsuitable, it is probably not true and anyway, that is not a reason to change your mind. Different families, different rules! If you are managing older children then including them in the process of deciding the family rules is an absolute must. They need to understand the reasons for the rules, which might be that the more they look at screens, the less physically active they are and that can lead to health/ weight problems, or the more they watch screens, the more likely this will interfere with their sleep. Rules can include:

- No phone use/texting during meals, at home or in restaurants.
- No television or screen use during mealtimes.
- The computer stays in a living area, downstairs.
- No screens/electronic devices in the bedrooms.
- All devices are turned off an hour before bedtime, there is evidence that the light from screens interferes with the onset of sleep.
- With teenagers, establishing a time when phones are switched off and handed over, not only reduces excessive use, but it also protects your teen from the excessive incoming phone use by peers.
- Set a limit to screen time, most experts agree that two hours a day is a reasonable limit.

If you set rules, then they need to be for everyone, and that includes the adults. Children learn more from watching what we do than listening to what we say.

3. School matters

Attachment is an innate behavioural and emotional system designed to maintain physical and emotional proximity between a developmentally immature infant and his or her caretakers. From the point of view of an observer, it is marked by proximity seeking. For the infant, it is marked by signs of emotional security. Attachment can be expressed through an intimate persisting affectional relationship, which between the dependent infant and their attachment figure, has a primary status and a biological function in development, (Cairns 2002).

Some children have attachment difficulties caused by absent, rejecting or multiple caretakers in their early life, or by institutional care, or on account of neglect/ abusive experiences. All children in the Looked After System and who are adopted, have had disrupted childhoods. Their experiences will have undermined, and perhaps may continue to undermine, the extent to which their needs are met and their development enhanced.

Risk factors

Disrupted childhoods stem from risk factors, which undermine development and wellbeing. These risk factors may include:

- Genetic influences.
- Environmental factors, e.g. poverty and deprivation, homelessness.
- Abuse, neglect or inadequate parenting.
- Parental substance abuse which limits parenting.
- Parents with physical or mental health problems, whereby a child's needs are not met.
- Family breakdown or parental conflict.
- Domestic abuse/ violence.
- Children with a physical and/or learning disability without appropriate support.
- Children from conflict zones.

The consequences can be, children with emotional or behavioural problems, Children demonstrating problems at school, children or young persons misusing alcohol or drugs, and children or young persons offending.

(Institute of Public Care, Bath (2003) Review of services to promote children's mental health and emotional well-being in Oxfordshire).

Disruptive factors

Understanding the kinds of disruption they have had to face, leads us to be able to plan more effectively to support children in school.

These children have experienced numerous, and often unplanned, moves of home. The move from their family of origin for whatever reason, disrupts their sense of who they are in the context of their family.

Siblings may have moved too, with the child or separately. The reactions of each child will be different. When siblings haven't moved, their links are disrupted by time and distance. It will take hard work on the part of carers/ professionals to establish contact, which can contribute to restoring a sense of kinship for the children.

The moves usually mean a break with extended family members, friends, neighbours and their local community. This undermines the child's sense of security and social well-being.

The process by which the child has come to be in the Looked After System or adopted, will have had its own impact on the child. There will have been: experiences that prompted intervention, the anxieties around accommodation/ care/adoption; and the changes to the child's world; these will be disruptions.

Only the children know the real details of their histories. They are often not able to have the insight to recount these, even to themselves. Their histories have shaped their personalities, learning styles, behaviours and their world views. It is often these manifestations of their history that we see in school.

Some early placements are temporary and/or short-term, such that neither the child nor the carers invest in a continuous, dependable relationship. For some children, much needed work on early experiences may be postponed until a more permanent placement is found. This leaves the child and the carers/ teachers struggling to understand the meaning of what has happened. Children need this work to be done to assess their difficulties and enhance their understanding, otherwise wrong assumptions may be made about the child's emotional state.

The moves of placement for a child rarely coincide with the common entry points to school such as a start in reception class, or the move to the junior school, or secondary school transfer. Any changes of school are difficult, but for children who are looked after/ adopted, who have moved to a new placement, she/he is also having to cope with the reasons that prompted the move and trying to fit into a family too. The change of school can plunge a child into a school setting in a way which is highly visible and which can leave a child feeling like an intruder.

There may be complexities of relationships within a placement. There may have to be a balance to be struck between the children in the home. There can be biological children/grandchildren, the child concerned, siblings and other foster/adopted children.

The needs of black and ethnic minority children may not be adequately provided for and this, then adds to the extent that the child feels she/ he can't get the validation they so much need, in the midst of disruption in their life.

Given the children's experiences of disrupted care, they all need individual care and support. Some of the children may have had several moves of school or time out of school. Lack of continuity will have undermined their progress in school and left them less able to make relationships with teachers and trust in their guidance. Mistrust can act as a barrier to educational success and the enjoyment of school.

Some of the children have identified special educational needs, such as dyslexia, attention problems and autism. In addition to these special needs, there may be barriers to providing effectively for their needs, such as moves of placement/schools and the consequent difficulties of assessment, effective interagency liaison, and understanding of the child's behaviour. Carers may need help to understand all the child's special educational needs, access the appropriate professional help, and secure resources to support the child in school.

What can be even more difficult is when a child has had adverse early experiences, moves of placement/school, and has unidentified special educational needs, If too much is made of the child's disrupted childhood, then the recognition of the real extent of the child's special needs can be at best delayed, and at worst overlooked completely. Managing with the impact of a disrupted childhood may mask other difficulties. Attachment difficulties rarely explain all the difficulties a child might have.

When children have had a lack of continuity in care and schooling, it can be particularly difficult for them to make and sustain relationships with peers. Some of the children have experienced bullying, racial abuse, and isolation, which compounds their difficulties and detracts from their self esteem still further.

What can schools offer?

Schools have a great deal to offer to children who have had disrupted childhoods. As a starting point, as parents/carers, we need to understand what schools offer:

- A place away from the experiences of the past and the closeness of family life. A neutral ground, away from painful areas.

- A world where the child can assume a meaningful role in a predictable, child-centred environment.

- Daily contact with concerned adults who model an interest in development learning and problem solving.

- Opportunities to learn to make relationships with peers and adults, and particularly to make and sustain friendships.

- Routines and structures in which to build personal confidence and social skills.

- Structured learning geared to provide experiences of success and to build self esteem.

- A system which has support agencies and networks, that can be used to provide counselling and support for personal problems.

- An introduction to what are hopefully life-long learning, interests and hobbies.

- Opportunities and achievements which are a gateway to adult life and the world of employment.

For children who have had disrupted childhoods, school can be a safe path, providing access to learning, personal development, independence and success.

Resilience factors

For children with disrupted childhoods, school can be a safe path, providing access to learning, development, independence and success. We do know that there are protective factors, which enhance development and contribute to children feeling good:

- Resilient temperament (biological resilience).
- Children with good health and development.
- Children with good problem-solving skills/coping strategies.
- Children with positive relationships with parents and for boys, good levels of involvement in parenting by fathers as a protective factor for offending, depression and suicidal thoughts.
- Parent or carer interest in the child's activities, including school.
- Supportive and involved grandparents.
- Access to high quality early-years education.
- Children with a pro-social peer group.
- Children attending a school with a 'good ethos' - minimal bullying.
- Children with access to challenging activities in and out of school.
- Supportive local community.

Institute of Public Care, Bath (2003). Review of services to promote children's mental health and emotional well-being in Oxfordshire.

Changing schools

There will be times when you consider, or may have to move your child from one school to another. This may worry you, as you will be mindful of the disruptions your child has already had to manage. Remember that what your child may have experienced in the past is sudden, unplanned moves, in adverse circumstances, with little support. Children need to learn to manage change and it is your job as parents to help them to do that. What follows is a framework for a move of school, which you might find helpful.

Moving School: What does it take to make inclusion work for your child?

1. Before the move	
More likely to be included	**Less likely to be included**
• The move of school is planned in advance.	• The move is sudden and unplanned.
• Support agencies/professionals provide records of their involvement/assessment.	• Paperwork contains no current assessment.
• Child has a stable home/carer situation.	• The move coincides with a change in the home circumstances for the child.
• The move of school entails a move to a school which is similar in terms of type/size/catchment/provision.	• The move involves very different education provision.
• The SENCO in the receiving school is involved in the plan and feels she/he has the time/resources to make appropriate arrangements.	• The SENCO is not told of the move until it happens.
• There is time to inform and involve all the staff, teaching and non-teaching, in planning for the inclusion of the pupil.	• None of the staff are aware of the background and the needs of the pupil who joins the school.
• Agencies/professionals which serve the receiving school are alerted before the move and if need be, meet to contribute to the plan for inclusion.	• The support agencies find out about pupil joining the school after she/he has arrived.

• There is a clear plan for the move with a timetable of integration support, realistically geared to the child's age/ stage/ abilities/ needs.	• The child arrives with little or no notice.
• The child understands what the move entails and wants to try to succeed in a different school setting.	• The move of school has been prompted by circumstances, which mean the child has no choice.

2. The move	
• The parent/carer has some insight into the difficulties the move of school has for the child.	• The parent/carer underestimates the implications of a move of school for the child.
• The parent/carer has good experiences of school.	• The parent/carer had bad experiences of school/has significant learning difficulties/ literacy difficulties/mental health problems.
• The parent/carer supports the school.	• The parent/carer does not prioritise support for the school.
• If the child has special educational needs, there is an up-to-date, full assessment of these. Otherwise, there is a record of the child's achievements in school.	• There is inadequate or no paperwork with regard to the child's achievements to date and current needs.
• If the child has special educational needs, there is appropriate and adequate support available when the child arrives.	• The school has a shortage of permanent teachers/teaching assistants, such that there will be a significant delay in providing appropriate and adequate support to meet the child's needs.
• The school has experience of successfully including children with special educational needs or who have to move in difficult circumstances (such as asylum seekers, children from refuges, children in public care).	• The school has a settled school population and is usually over subscribed and has little experience of children moving to the school due to difficult circumstances.
• There is a plan and support for a gradual programme for an inclusion with a built-in review process and contingency plans.	• There is an expectation that the move will work or not work.

• The nature of the education provision is similar to what the child has previously experienced in terms of class size, curriculum, support.	• The move entails the child being placed in very different provision from previously.
• The move of school does not disrupt sibling/friendship relationships in the child's community.	• The move totally disrupts sibling/ friendship relationships, so the child has not got established ties with peers in the community.

3. Monitoring the child	
• There is a named person in the school who oversees the plan for inclusion.	• No one person on the staff is able to oversee the child settling in to the school.
• The child has an identified adult in school to whom she/he can go if there are difficulties.	• There are no contingency plans in place.
• The parent/carer is actively involved in monitoring how the child settles, initially on a daily, then weekly, then half-termly basis.	• The parent/carer is only contacted by the school, when something goes wrong in school.
• The school is prepared to be flexible about arrangements.	• The school takes the view that if the plan doesn't work, then the child's needs cannot be met in school.
• There are planned reviews of the plan to include the child, which involve the parent/carer, staff and the child together, with the relevant professionals from support agencies.	• No plans are made to review the arrangements.
• Lessons learnt from the plan to include the child, are incorporated into the school's policy and practice with regard to inclusion.	• The school sees the inclusion of the child as a matter of individual needs/personality. Systems and practices in the school remain unchanged.

What teachers can do to support looked after/ adopted children

Be accepting of care/ adoption - Families have changed over the years. Teachers can do a great deal if they set an ethos of acceptance for a range of family structures. They can demonstrate this by including alternative family arrangements when they talk about families, inherited characteristics, and care for children. The school could recognise Adoption Day, and be open to celebrating with the child and family their own special days, such as the day the adoption was finalised. Teachers need to use the term 'birth' parents, rather than 'natural' or 'real' parents. These latter terms can seem to imply that other arrangements are unnatural or unreal.

Reinforce a sense of belonging - Children who are in care or are adopted, have had disruptions in their opportunities to build secure relationships. Teachers can signal their support to a child by promoting their feelings of being accepted and belonging in school. They could greet the child by name in the morning, and try hard to end each day on a positive note.

Build self esteem - Children who have had disrupted childhoods may have had little experience of being positively noticed and validated. They might find it hard to believe and accept praise. Teachers can help by giving low key, genuine praise. The teacher should not be put off by a negative or rejecting response from the child. All this shows is the extent of the child's need to build up a different and positive view of themselves.

Check the curriculum - Some of the curriculum content will identify children in alternative family arrangements as different and could make them feel uncomfortable and not accepted. Work on family histories, family trees, Mother's/ Father's day, baby photographs, biographies and family holidays, can, if not handled sensitively, be excluding at least and distressing at worst. It helps if teachers can discuss the curriculum with the child's parents, so ways to include the child are planned and so that they can prepare the child beforehand.

Organisation issues - Many children who have disrupted childhoods have not had adult models of reliable child-centred organisation. Rather than comment on the child who struggles with organisation issues, the teacher can provide strategies, which enable the child to be more organised and more able to take increased responsibility. Strategies such as: clear, consistent classroom routines, simple displays of visual prompts, allowing more time and pairing the child with a child who will model being organised.

Kind discipline - When children show signs of difficulties and their behaviour begins to be a concern, much can be done by stepping in early. A child may be helped by the teacher taking responsibility, such as 'I didn't explain that well'; giving strategies to manage such as 'I find it helps doing this to... '; and providing a safe space for the child to regain self control before all is lost, such as 'can you just sit and hold this for me and then we can....'.

Anticipate/ be aware of bullying - It may be that the teacher over hears intrusive questions being asked by peers or sees a change in who sits by whom. If the teacher has previously talked to the family, she/ he can be aware of the family ideas about dealing with unwelcome questions. The teacher can then step in to help the child being questioned in much the same way that they might do for children being singled out by peers about divorce in families or race issues. Adopted children's feelings about their families are at the core of their vulnerabilities and being. They will need help to protect that core.

Be mindful of the need to use space sensitively - For children who have been unhappy previously, being in a confined space not of their choosing can be distressing and trigger memories which they may not be able to understand and contain. On the other hand, some children may need a secure space to be in if they feel anxious. They may need to build round themselves with cushions.

Homework - Homework takes some accepting by pupils and managing by parents. Children and parents have to learn this and develop strategies whereby it is done. Homework can be a particular difficulty for children who have had disrupted childhoods. It increases the pressures at home, when the family already has much to adjust to and manage. Teachers can help with homework in terms of, making sure the tasks set are understood by the child, they are easily achievable, positive, and are an aid to learning.

Talking to the family - The family may be caring for or have adopted the child and been brought suddenly into contact with schools. They will need information about school systems and routines, so they can support their child. They may feel apart from other parents not having a shared experience with them of being parents of a child in the school. They might feel like other parents know the school or the teachers better. They may be dealing with 'instant' parenthood; or the placement of more than one child, perhaps children with competing needs, and have a less well-established support network for themselves as parents. Teachers need to check with the family whether there are confidentiality issues which the school could inadvertently breach by: class lists; displays of work by named children; or photographs of children displayed in school or outside school. There could be matters of safeguarding the child, in terms of phone calls, which may be made to school, or visits to school, by members of the child's family of origin.

The teacher should be prepared to ask for support - The histories of children in care and who are adopted are complex and difficult. Every child is unique in her/his experiences of adversity. As parents you will have done adoption preparation courses, had social work support, and be grappling with your child's issues every day. A gentle reminder to your child's teacher that you understand that your child is vulnerable and that this can add to what she/he has to manage, will reassure them and make it more, rather than less likely that the teacher will ask for help. It can be that your local Adoption team can provide support to you and the teacher to work things out to the benefit of your child in school.

Self esteem

We have just taken an eight year old boy to live with us. He was living with his mum before he came to us. She has mental health problems. She has suffered from depression for years. She has also got problems as she drinks heavily and she wasn't able to care for him and support him in school. He is clearly very bright, but he has difficulties making friends in school, he gets into fights in the playground, and his progress is slow. I think he needs extra help in school and I have asked for this. What can we do at home to help him?

Foster Carers

There is a lot that the school can do to help him. You can be sure that the Special Educational Needs Co-ordinator will be considering how the school can support him. Your support is an essential component of this work.

It is likely that he has been neglected, confused by his mum's difficulties, and he has not had the support he needed to attend school regularly and make progress.

Children have physical, emotional, social and intellectual needs. Those needs must be met if they are to thrive. These needs are inter-related, for example an unhappy baby may not eat, and even if the baby eats, it may not thrive. The child who is faced with criticism and inconsistency, cannot learn how to behave, and is more likely to be fearful and anxious. When a child lives with violence and aggression, she/he can feel worthless, unworthy of care and may treat others accordingly. Children with low self esteem do not do well in school:

- They don't believe they can do well and they are reluctant to try when faced with new things and when tasks appear to them to be difficult.

- They have difficulties making trusting relationships with teachers. Mistrust can act as a barrier to educational success and the enjoyment of school.

- They struggle to make and sustain friendships with peers and can be rejected socially.

- They find the good order of schools as serving to emphasise their powerlessness and they can feel driven to challenge the authority of well meaning adults.

- Their anxieties may be such that they are not intellectually curious and ready to learn, preferring to focus on self preservation rather than learning.

Children need to feel loved and valued, if they are to build a positive sense of self esteem. Parents/carers can help in the following ways:

- Provide love
  A stable, continuous, dependable loving relationship with parents/ carers is a basis on which a child can learn she/he is valued and valuable. It is on the basis of being loved that a child builds self esteem and learns to love others.

- Promote security
  Children are helped by having stable, secure family relationships, reliable routines and familiar settings, where they feel safe. When a child knows continuity and predictability, she/he has a base from which to venture into new and challenging situations.

- Offer new experiences
  Children need to learn how to learn. To do this, they need new experiences, which are appropriate to their age and stage of development. The cry of a two year old 'me do it' signals the joy, sense of achievement and emotional well-being, that children get from the mastery of new skills. Children of all ages need new experiences, which are carefully chosen to maximise their experiences of success.

- Give praise and recognition
  When significant adults, especially parents/carers, give a child praise for their achievements, the child feels encouraged and her/his self esteem is enhanced. It is very important to recognise and praise effort, as well as success. We know that children can learn from making mistakes, as well as from being successful. They need to have positive self regard, if they are to try new tasks and risk failure.

- Allow for responsibility
  With age appropriate responsibility, children learn to develop personal independence. For this, children need a framework of guidance, boundaries and support, in which they can practise being responsible and independent. To do this, children need to feel good about themselves and able to make mistakes safely and without fear.

All of this takes time and the commitment of adults. You can only take each day as it comes and provide what you can, to build a positive sense of self esteem in your child. In all this, do not neglect your own need for nurturing and support.

4. The Role of the Designated Teacher

Every school has to have a Designated Teacher with responsibilities for children who are in the Looked After System (Section 20 of the Children and Young Persons Act 2008). The school's governing body is expected to ensure that the post is held by a qualified teacher with appropriate training. (www.dcsf.gov.uk). The establishment of these posts has promoted the need to build up knowledge and expertise with regard to this very special group of children and young people. Currently this does now include adopted children, this member of staff is the person who may be most receptive to the need to support adopted children in school. Their role includes the following:

- **Learning about the care system,** the impact of being in care on education, legal responsibilities and associated guidance for support to children and young people. She/he is expected to be aware of the emotional, psychological and social effects of loss and separation from birth families.

- **Liaising with Social Workers and other agencies** to help your child with the initial transition into the school, and both you and your child with continued communication with the school. This teacher is a key contact person for you as parents/carers. She/he needs to be aware of the child's present situation and any changes that may occur.

- **Ensuring that there are clear lines of communication about your child's needs,** both within the school and with the professional network around the child. Systems can be in place to help with this, such as the space for parent comments in your child's school planner or the effective use of school support staff.

- **Promoting inclusive policies** and helpful pastoral systems in the school for children who are in care, who have had disrupted childhoods and previous unhappy or unsuccessful experiences of schools.

- **Providing links between parents/carers and the school** for home-school agreements and the establishment of current useful Personal Education Plans. In particular, she/he can help you to support your child at school.

- **Promoting an ethos of realistic high expectations** with regard to your child's achievements in learning and in social behaviour. The teacher can act as an advocate for your child in the school.

- **Being alert to difficulties that your child may be having in school** and working to support appropriate interventions as early as is possible. This may include consulting with you with regard to involving Education support agencies to advise school staff and ensuring that special educational needs are assessed without delay.

- **Maintaining records of your child** with due respect for the need for confidentiality, while being clear when information needs to be shared. The teacher should ensure that information is shared sensitively on a need to know basis.

- **Acting as a resource for other staff** with regard to differentiated teaching strategies appropriate for individual children. The teacher ensures that the needs of children in care are kept on the agenda of the school as policies and practices are developed.

Much depends on the nature of the appointment and the type of school. In Primary schools, the Designated Teacher can be the Headteacher, the Deputy Headteacher, the Special Educational Needs Co-ordinator (SENCO) or the Designated Teacher for Safeguarding, and some are several of these in one person. In large Secondary schools, the role is less likely to be a combined one. This post demands that a teacher take on a lead role on behalf of the most disadvantaged and complex children in the system; children, who can challenge the school system. It can be difficult to combine the roles of teaching and advocacy.

Common areas of difficulties arise when:

- The child is placed in the school without the teachers being given all the relevant information.

- The teachers have difficulties contacting a parent/carer and/or social worker about concerns or difficulties.

- There are misunderstandings between agencies which impact on the day-to-day management of your child in school.

- The Personal Education Plan for a child is late and/or not realistic and helpful, (see Chapter 5).

- Lack of notification of the need to change placements and the reasons behind the moves.

The work of the Virtual School

I am a teacher in a primary school. The Head has just asked me if I would take on the post of Designated Teacher for Children who are in the Looked After System. I don't remember having been taught about children in care/adopted when I was training, so I am worried that I don't have enough information and experience to do the job well. I think one of my strengths as a teacher is that I think about the whole child, not just what I see of a child in school, and I want to learn more. I would like to do the job. Is there support for me doing this?

Class Teacher

Thinking about the whole child, and especially trying to understand the impact of the child's history, is a great place to start. The job of the Designated Teacher for children in the Looked After System is demanding, interesting and can be very rewarding. An ability to work alongside other professionals is a must. There will be times when it will seem to be complicated, challenging and time consuming work.

Most Local Authorities have dedicated teams who support schools with the task of raising the educational achievements of children in school who are also in the Looked After System. Following the publication of Care Matters in 2008 the government asked all Local Authorities to appoint a Virtual Headteacher to support and challenge all professionals concerned with the education of Looked After Children in order to raise aspiration and achievement. This has led, in Oxfordshire and many other areas, to the setting up of a Virtual School for Looked After Children. This team supports Designated Teachers, Foster Carers, Social Workers and other partners in the following ways:

- Monitoring, advice and support for staff to complete Personal Education Plans, with guidance and possible offers of short term financial support from the Personal Education Allowance (PEA).

- In-Service training for small/whole staff groups on a range of topics such as: the work of the Virtual School, behaviour problems, attachment, joint agency work, Personal Education Plans.

- Literacy projects to boost work in schools for children in care: Reading Quest and Letterbox.

- Advice on assessments from a Special Needs Advisory Teacher (SNAST) for teachers of children in primary schools or who are new into care.

- Short term interventions from education mentors for some individual children in primary schools.

- Specialist teachers for Key Stages 1/2 and 3/4, where there are specific needs to be addressed with regard to a child's learning in school.

- Learning Mentors for some pupils in Key Stages 2 and 3, and for pupils in Key Stage 4 who need help to access the National Curriculum, complete coursework and revise for examinations.

- Monitoring of attainment and achievement in order to ensure appropriate support and intervention is in place.

- Advice and support from a teacher with the Behaviour Support Service, who can provide input to staff in schools where a child in the Looked After System has emotional or behavioural difficulties.

- Consultation Meetings to support schools and parents/carers where a child in the Looked After System has difficulties in school, which are beyond the scope of the usual school support agencies.

- Liaison with alternative education provision, such as Pupil Referral Units, with regard to children in care who need their specialist support.

- Support to parent/carers and residential staff to promote reading, access to reading materials and library resources.

- Regular Psychology Service input to Foster Carers' support groups on a wide range of issues.

- Regular support and advice about education from Virtual School staff to those in residential settings in order to raise the achievement of the children in their care.

- Publications prepared for children, parents/carers and teachers which provide information and enhance understandings about children in the Looked After System and their education:

    o Support in schools: people and what they do (for children/young people).
    o Attachment and the consequences of disrupted childhood.
    o The Adopted Child in school.
    o Guarding against the misuse of computers and the Internet to abuse children and young people.
    o Life Story Work booklet.

- Support for home access to ICT including projects providing laptops and ICT e-safety training.

- Advice on school placement, admissions, exclusion and attendance.

5. Personal education plans

All children in the Looked After System must have a care plan, which is drawn up and reviewed by the Local Authority. The care plan identifies intended outcomes and objectives for the child and carers with regard to the child's development, identity, relationships and self care skills. The care plan must include a health plan and a Personal Education Plan, (PEP). The PEP is part of the official school record of a child in the Looked After System. Personal Education Plans are a process, whereby all the adults supporting a child in the Looked After System, can talk to each other and make educational plans that make a difference to the child's life chances.

Unlike other children, you know that there are more adults involved in your child's care. This can add complexities to achieving a shared understanding of roles and expectations with regard to your child's educational needs. The PEP is a vital document because it provides a 'collective memory' about education. An effective PEP should:

- Identify developmental and educational needs in relation to skills, knowledge, subject areas and experiences.

- Set short and long term educational attainment targets agreed in partnership with the child and you as carer.

- Be a record of planned actions, for example with regard to homework, extra tuition, study support and any specific plans made to promote the educational achievement of your child.

- Include information on how the progress of your child is to be rigorously monitored.

- Record details of specific interventions and targeted support that will be used to make sure personal education targets are met. One-to-one tuition can have a significant impact on progress and this should be employed whenever appropriate, as one of the key strategies for raising attainment.

- Say what will happen or is already happening to put in place any additional support which may be required, for example, actions to support special educational needs.

- Set out how a child's aspirations, self confidence and ambition, is being nurtured, especially in consideration of longer term goals towards further and higher education, work experience and career plans.

- Be a record of your child's academic achievements and her/his participation in the wider activities of the school and other out of school learning activities, (sport, personal development, community groups).

- Provide information which helps all who are supporting your child's educational achievement, to understand what works best.

- Have a clear explanation of accountability in terms of who, within the school, is responsible for making the actions identified in the PEP happen.

Some children in the Looked After System have an Education Health and Care plan (EHCP) (see chapter 6). If this is the case for your child, you will find that the PEP will include the relevant information from the EHCP and annual reviews of the Plan. What follows is a quick guide to the PEP process:

Ten point quick guide to Personal Education Plans

1. **Personal Education Plans (PEPs) are a statutory part of social care for all children in the Looked After System, regardless of age and education setting and are reviewed every six months.** This includes babies, all school age children, and young people who have left school. They may be in education, employment, training or unemployed.

2. **The child's Social Worker is responsible for ensuring that there is a PEP within 20 days, for all children new into care or new to a school setting (i.e. transferring between schools).** This is useful, as it means the Social Worker alerts the school to the child's Looked After status and begins the PEP process of bringing everyone together. The PEP meeting is chaired by the Designated Teacher.

3. **Thereafter, the school's Designated Teacher for Children in the Looked After System has the responsibility for all PEP meetings and paperwork.** There is a named Designated Teacher in all schools. Once the PEP is in place, she/he has the task of calling a meeting, reviewing the plan, and ensuring the paperwork is completed.

4. **Meetings should include the Designated Teacher, Social Worker, Carer, the birth parent if appropriate, the child, education support professionals if deemed to be useful.** All the adults who support the child should be invited.

5. **The PEP documentation has three main parts:**
    (i) **The Core Document which, once complete, needs updating each meeting.**
    (ii) **The school year group review form.**
    (iii) **The form for the child's view.**

    The documentation for the PEP meetings will be on the Local Authority website and can be accessed, by professionals employed by the Local Authority, carers can telephone or email the Virtual School to get copies of the documents and/or advice with regard to an individual child's PEP.

6. **The meetings should focus on all aspects of educational development in school and out of school.** This includes how the child copes in

school with the work, their behaviour and social relationships. It also includes school clubs, community activities, and particular talents/interests of the child. The paperwork has been designed to guide discussions.

7. **At each PEP meeting, targets are set for the child or the adults who support the child.** Subsequent review meetings discuss whether the targets have been met and any new targets that are felt to be appropriate and useful.

   Targets must be smart i.e.
   Specific
   Measurable
   Achievable
   Realistic
   Timed.

8. **Ideas for targets are:** Improving reading levels by, raising self-esteem/friendships, by joining activities/clubs, strategies to improve behaviour, ensuring support is in place to improve educational progress/ behaviour/ emotional or social development, developing a particular interest/talent, providing time/resources to nurture a child.

9. **When the child has an Education Health and Care Plan (EHCP)** their progression in school is closely monitored and regularly reviewed in termly review meetings. This is lead by the Special Education Needs Co-ordinator, (SENCO) and includes the child, the parent/carer, and the professional network. To avoid unnecessary duplication the Annual SEN Review meeting and paperwork can be one of the two PEP meetings required for the child in a given year.

10. **The PEP meeting may identify a need for some specific short-term support for a child, which requires funding:** such as additional support for a term to aid transition, or for a piece of equipment; or for counselling or emotional support. An application for funding will only be considered if there is a current PEP in place. When funding is given, the school is asked to report on how it was used and evaluate the impact of the support.

    When children cease to be in the Looked After System (for example because they are adopted or are subject to a Special Guardianship Order), their educational needs are unlikely to have changed significantly with the change in care status. While there will not be a statutory requirement that they have a PEP, Designated Teachers can consider continuing the process, if it is felt this will significantly contribute to meeting a child's education needs.

    For more detailed guidance, any questions or queries about a child's education and/or the PEP process please contact your Local Authorities service for supporting children who are looked after or adopted.

PEP meetings

I have just been to a PEP meeting for the boy who lives with us. We have been under the impression that he was coping quite well in school. His Form Tutor has been quite positive about him, whenever we have spoken to her. You can imagine how confused we felt when we went to his PEP meeting and we were told about his inappropriate behaviour in some lessons and that he has outstanding detentions.

Foster Father

Oh dear, it sounds like the communication between his Form Tutor and his subject teachers has not been as good as it needs to be, to give you a balanced picture of how he is managing in school. PEP meetings are a process whereby all the adults supporting a child in the Looked After System, can talk to each other, celebrate the achievements of the child and make positive educational plans for the next six months. You need to know if there are difficulties, and it is not helpful to you or your child if you first hear of these in the PEP meeting. Here are some ideas to discuss with the school:

- If the school has not already done so, ask if the Form Tutor or Designated Teacher for Children who are Looked After can get a 'round robin' of staff views. This is an informal way of collecting the opinions of staff with regard to concerns about an individual child. Have a look at this with staff, to see if the problems are general or specific to particular lessons/teachers. Discuss this with your child and with staff with a view to considering what strategies might help.

- In busy secondary schools, it is important to have a key person who will maintain contact between home and the different members of staff who deal with the child. This can help to avoid a situation of conflicting messages.

- Ask if you can establish a regular time and form of contact between home and school, at a frequency which works for staff and you as parents/carers. Regular contact is much better than contact when things go wrong and feelings are running high! When there are difficulties, waiting until the next PEP meeting will be too long.

- Check with the school with regard to the levels of support that can be offered either to the child or to staff teaching the child. If the difficult behaviour is entrenched, then it is usual for school staff to have planned their intervention in the form of a Pastoral Support Plan. You will be involved in this.

- Discuss with the school whether professionals from the Education Support Agencies need to be involved.

- If the child has an Educational Health and Care Plan (EHCP), then it might be useful to the staff or to you as a parent/carer, to consider requesting the involvement of the school's Educational Psychologist in a review of the situation/support in school.

- It may be that the school and you as parents/carers would welcome the advice and support of the Virtual School about the PEP or their presence at a future meeting. Discuss this with the staff and agree who will contact the Virtual School.

6. Special educational needs

What is Special Educational Needs (SEN) Support?

All children learn in different ways and make differing rates of progress.

Some children find learning harder than others, perhaps in reading, writing, maths or developing social skills and may need more help and support to make progress.

If it is the case that a child has greater difficulty in learning than most of the children of the same age or needs support that is additional or different to the others in their class, then they are said to have special educational needs (SEN). The legal definition of SEN has not changed.

If the early years setting, school or college your child or young person attends thinks your child may have special educational needs (SEN), they must talk to you about it.

Most children with special educational needs and disabilities (SEND) are educated in their local mainstream school and should be given support with their learning to help them make progress. The support they are given is called SEN Support and is defined as 'help that is additional to or different from the support generally given to most of the other children of the same age'.

The school or setting should always let you know and involve you in decisions before they start giving the extra or different help to your child.

They should also discuss with you any plans to reduce or remove support from your child.

Who decides whether my child needs SEN Support?

All class and subject teachers should regularly check whether their pupils are making progress. If they think your child is finding it harder than others to make progress, they should consider whether they might have SEN or need additional or different support from the others in the class.

The school should talk to you and your child about this. If a young person is 16 or older, the school should involve them directly.

Sometimes you may be the first to be aware that your child has some special educational needs. If you think your child may need SEN Support, you should talk to your child's teacher or to the Special Educational Needs Co-ordinator (SENCO).

Every school is required to identify and address the SEN of all pupils in their school and must do their best to make sure that any child with SEN gets the support they need.

If you are not happy about the support your child has, you can ask to talk to the SENCO or head teacher. If you feel you need help, advice or support for this meeting at school, you can contact SENDIASS or parent support services within your local authority.

Schools use guidance documents **SEN Support** to help them decide whether and what type of support your child needs.

These help to make sure that all schools and settings have a clear and consistent approach to identifying when a child or young person has SEN and how to support them to achieve good outcomes. They set out how parents, children and young people should be involved in decision-making, as well as what schools and settings are expected to put in place for pupils with SEN from the funding that they receive.

This guidance is helpful in looking at the individual needs of each child and suggesting a range of approaches to meet their particular need.

The checklists in this guidance are intended to help identify a child's level of need and are not criteria. There is no specific number of ticks required to access SEN Support.

The SEND Code of Practice

The Code tells schools, Local Authorities and a long list of other organisations how to put the changes in SEN and Disability law contained within the Children and Families Act 2014 into practice.

It is statutory guidance and says what they **must** do and also what they **should** do. The difference between must and should is the 'musts' have to be done and 'should 'means that they have to consider following the guidance and if they don't, have a good reason for not doing so.

A graduated approach

Because children and young people learn in different ways and can have different kinds or levels of SEN, the SEN Support system uses a graduated approach. This means that increasingly, step-by-step, specialist expertise can be brought in to help the early years setting, school or college with the difficulties that a child or young person may have.

The approach may include:

- an individually-designed learning programme.
- extra help from a teacher/tutor or teaching assistant (TA).
- being taught individually or in a small group for regular short periods.
- making or changing materials and equipment.

- drawing up a personal plan, including setting targets for improvement, and a regular review of progress before setting new targets.
- advice and/or extra help from specialists such as specialist teachers, educational psychologists, and therapists.

The early years setting, school or college should include you in any discussions, and should consider your views, and the views of your son or daughter, in making any decisions about how best to help your child. They should keep you informed about your child's progress.

If your child does not make enough progress, the teacher/tutor or the Special Educational Needs Co-ordinator (SENCO) should then talk to you about asking for advice from outside professionals, for example, an educational psychologist **(EP),** a specialist teacher or a speech and language therapist (SALT) or other health professionals.

The **SEND Code of Practice** says that a school can ask for this advice at any point, but should always involve a specialist where a pupil continues to work at levels substantially below others in their class or make little or no progress, despite receiving appropriate support delivered by appropriately trained staff.

The **SEND Code of Practice** says that when your child is identified as having SEN, the school should take action to remove barriers to learning and put effective special educational provision in place. This SEN support should take the form of a four-part cycle:

1. Assess

Every school has to have a Special Educational Needs Co-ordinator (SENCO). The SENCO has day-to-day responsibility for how children with SEN are supported within a school and to co-ordinate the specific provision for individual pupils. The SENCO must be a qualified teacher and will work with teaching staff to assess your child's needs, so that they receive the right support. They should involve you in this and take your concerns seriously and, where possible, seek your child's views.

Sometimes schools will seek advice from a specialist teacher or a health professional. They should talk to you about this first.

2. Plan

If the school decides that your child needs SEN Support, it **must** tell you. The school should agree with you the outcomes that will be set, what help will be provided and a date when you can see/check what progress there has been.

3. Do

Your child's class or subject teacher is responsible for the work that is done with your child, and should work closely with any teaching assistants or specialist staff involved. The school should tell you who is responsible for the support your child receives.

The school should record the outcomes, actions and support agreed with you and your child. These should be shared with all those who work with your child so that they are aware of their needs, the outcomes that were agreed and any teaching strategies and approaches that are needed. These records are a good starting point for discussions about how your child is doing at school.

The Local Authority will also always want to have this information if they are asked to carry out an assessment of your child's needs.

4. Review

The school should review your child's progress, and the difference that the help your child has been given has made, on the date agreed in the plan. You and your child should be involved in the review and in planning the next steps.

The **SEND Code of Practice** says that schools should meet parents at least three times per year. These meetings should allow sufficient time for you to express your view, to discuss and plan effectively, so would be longer than most parent-teacher meetings.

If your child has not made progress in spite of having received extra support, the review should decide what could be done next. This may include more or different help.

You might feel that your child is not making progress in spite of any additional support or that the gap between them and others in their class is widening. If you disagree with the school on what progress has been made, you could ask the class teacher or SENCO to go through the SEN Support guidance with you and discuss any points where there is disagreement about what your child is finding difficult.

If other professionals have not already been involved, you might suggest that it might be helpful to approach them to help get a clearer picture of your child's difficulties or to plan the next steps.

You and the school can look on the Local Authority website at the Local Offer, which puts together a wide range of specialist and targeted services for children and young people with special education needs and disabilities.

Sometimes the next step may be to ask the local authority for an **Education Health and Care needs assessment.** If the school decides to do this, they must tell you. If you think it is needed, you can ask for it yourself.

How do I find out what the school provides for children who need SEN Support?

Every school must publish an **SEN information report** about the SEN provision the school makes. You can find this on the school's website.

This must include:

- How the school provides for children and young people with a wide range of special educational needs.
- The name of the school SENCO and how they can be contacted.
- Their SEN/Equality/Accessibility policies.
- How the school identifies children and young people with SEN and gives them extra help.
- How the school works with parents and children/young people..
- How the school adapts the curriculum for children and young people with SEN.
- What expertise and training the staff have in SEN.
- Which specialist support services the school uses.
- How the school checks the provision they make for their pupils with SEN is being effective.
- How children and young people with SEN are helped to access activities outside of the classroom.
- What the school does to support the wellbeing of children/young people with SEN.
- How the school prepares children for joining the school and moving on between schools and into adulthood.
- Who to contact if you are concerned about your child or wish to make a complaint.

You can also ask your child's teacher or the school's SENCO for information on the SEN provision made by the school.

Where can I get more information, advice or support?

You can find out more about SEN Support by:

- Looking at the SEN Information Report on the school website
- Talking to your child's teacher or the SENCO
- Looking at the Local Offer

You can also get in touch with SENDIASS who can give you:

- Information about SEN Support
- Advice about what to do if you are not happy with the support your school is providing
- Support at meetings at your child's school or setting
- Information about other organisations, support groups and information services that could help
- Information and advice about how to request an EHC needs assessment.

Sendiass can offer:

- A telephone helpline.
- Information, advice and support on matters to do with your child's SEN.
- Help with communication between you and the Local Authority.
- Trained volunteer Independent Parental Supporters and Independent Supporters.
- Advice about preventing and resolving disagreements.
- Training events for parents and groups - see SENDIASS website.
- An informal Drop in SEN Advice session, 'Talking Points', refer to website for dates.

This chapter was written by the Oxfordshire Special Educational Needs and Disability Information Advice and Support Service (SENDIASS). Most Local Authorities have a SENDIASS service or equivalent support.

Repeating a year in school

We are looking after our grand-daughter and we have Special Guardianship. She was born with Foetal Alcohol Syndrome and Neonatal Abstinence Syndrome; basically she was born having been affected in the womb by her mother's misuse of alcohol and heroin. Sadly, her mum is still not able to care for her as she continues to drink and take drugs. The Paediatrician says our grand-daughter is developmentally delayed and he doesn't know if she will catch up. She is behind her classmates even now and she is only 6 years old. We would like her to stay down a year, to give her more time to learn the basics and catch up. Is this a good idea, and who should we ask about this?

Grandmother

Your grand-daughter is lucky you are in a position to care for her. In the circumstances, it sounds like Special Guardianship was a wise decision. Your grand-daughter has special educational needs for which she will need support in school. Repeating a year is not going to help her much. If she isn't coping now, there is no reason to believe that repeating the year and doing more of the same, will help her cope. She needs to have a detailed assessment in school, with the class teacher being supported by the Special Educational Needs Co-ordinator (SENCO). This will provide them with a clear picture of her strengths and difficulties, and they can then use this to plan ways to help her. Schools take a staged approach to supporting children with special educational needs. This is laid out in a Code of Practice.

Special help for her can include:

- Differentiating the curriculum so she can understand what is taught.

- Giving her instructions, in a way which helps her retain what is expected of her, such as single step instructions or giving her visual prompts.

- Having a Teacher Assistant available to help her in the lessons she finds particularly difficult.

- Teaching her the basics of reading, writing and number work, in a small group for regular short periods, so the pace is right for her.

- Giving her more repetition to help her practise what she knows and remember it better.

- Making or changing materials and equipment to provide her with learning aids, such as Maths equipment or special computer software.

Then SENCO will write an Individual Education Plan (IEP) for her with achievable targets, so her progress can be monitored. If she doesn't make as much progress as you and the school hope, the school will involve professionals from Education Support Agencies, such as the Educational Psychology Service.

The school's Educational Psychologist might want to discuss your grand-daughter with you, do more assessment, discuss her with her teacher and make more suggestions about supporting her in school. If she later continues to need a high level of support, then the school will discuss her with you at the termly review meetings. Together you may end up considering whether she and the school would be helped by requesting a statutory assessment of her special needs, to see if she needs the support of an Education Health and Care Plan (EHCP).

I would suggest asking for a meeting with her class teacher to ask what the school plans to do to support your grand-daughter. If you want support and advice on the Code of Practice and the process of supporting your grand-daughter's special educational needs, contact the Special Educational Needs and Disability Information Advice and Support Service (SENDIASS).

7. Supporting children in school

Introduction

Once children are in the Looked After System or adopted, their parents/carers are naturally anxious to do everything they can to support the child. Just as you learn how to attune to your child, given her/his history, stage of development and strengths/difficulties; it is important to tune into the school and its demands. It will go well if you can see the teachers and the school as partners. You are special parents who have been assessed and trained, and who have ongoing professional support. You know your child and you are in a position to think about your child's experiences and the messages your child may have taken from what has happened. You will have insights, which you can share, on a need to know basis, with school staff. This will help the staff deal with your child in a more sensitive and effective way. The teachers will understand the school, its purposes and the learning process. So there will be times when they need to be giving you information and guidance. It is important to learn to be a parent/carer who is interested in and supportive of your child in school, while respecting and working with the teachers.

Here are some ideas:

- **Maintain regular routines at home with regard to sleep, meals, and having enjoyable leisure activities.**

    Starting school is a big step for small children. It means parting from parents/carers, initially for part of a day and then for the whole day. The familiar sights and sounds of home are replaced by the challenges of being part of a group, following routines, and organised teaching/learning. If your child has difficulties settling into school, tiredness, and at times, outbursts at home, these are signs of the efforts the child is having to make to adjust. For children in the Looked After System and who have been adopted, they have already had to cope with moves of home, and so these challenges at school are all the more difficult. Change for them in the past, may have meanings around feeling unloved, powerless, and upset. As a consequence, they will need more reassurance, nurturing and support.

    A move to secondary school can have an even greater impact on family life in lots of ways. The school may be further away, this may mean getting up earlier, having more things to organise and pack for the school day, with different requirements on different days, allowing time for the journey, and coming home with homework. For children who have had disrupted childhoods, coping with these demands may be particularly difficult. Their early care may have been such that they don't have practised organisation skills. However much you want to support your child at secondary school, it is important to remember that the biggest thing you can do to support your child is to maintain your home and family as a predictable, warm and supportive place to be. As your child faces the demands of secondary school, it is all the more important that she/he is certain that home offers a welcome, care and support.

- **Learn the names of key members of staff for your child.**

    In nursery and primary schools, it is easier to get to know most, if not all, the members of staff. The school settings are smaller and local. The dependence of small children is such that parents/carers usually take their children to and from school, and so you can have twice daily contact with the school staff. This is very helpful to children who have had experiences of inconsistency. They can see adults/parents/carers working together for their benefit.

    One of the most obvious changes for your child at secondary school will be the number of teachers that she/he has to deal with during each school day. From having one teacher all day, sometimes every day at primary school, your child will probably have a different teacher for each subject on the timetable. This may mean that she/he has to relate to up to six, or even as many as eight, different teachers in a day. Different subject lessons will be in different rooms, they call for different teaching methods and different teachers have their own styles: for example there will be a contrast between the discipline needed in a science laboratory and the freedom of expression in a drama studio. For some children in the Looked After System or who have been adopted, this is a particularly difficult feature of school. Changes of teacher style, learning situations and pupil expectations, can feel like unpredictability, which for them, brings feelings of insecurity.

    It is helpful if you can get to know the names of the members of staff who teach your child for all the different subjects. This demonstrates your interest, means you can listen to what they say about their day and you will be more clear about what has happened, and should you need to contact a teacher, you will be able to do so by name. It will be particularly helpful to know the name of your child's form tutor and head of year, both of whom may or may not teach your child.

- **Read the school's newsletters.**

    Do read them, as this again signals your interest in your child's experiences in school and they are a useful source of information. Many children in the Looked After System or who have been adopted, have had parents who were not successful in school and so were less able to have the confidence and literacy skills to manage school information. Reading the school's newsletters and discussing these with your child and family, puts you as a parent/carer in a position of having information, and this can help your child feel more secure.

    Most, if not all schools, produce newsletters in which they provide information for parents/carers and for the pupils in the school. You could ask about these when you visit the school before your child starts at the school and then you can be on the lookout for them once your child starts. Children in primary schools usually come out of school clutching these and are met by a parent/carer who can then be assured of a copy. It is probably the case that in the early months of starting at secondary school, your child may carefully bring these home to you. As most parents of children at secondary school will tell you, as time goes by, these are likely to lie crumpled and forgotten at the bottom of your child's school bag. A weekly bag search might be a good routine. The majority of schools now use e-mail to distribute newsletters.

- **Support the school rules.**

It will be the case either when you visited the school beforehand or when your child starts school, that you and your child have been provided with copies of the school rules. Schools are organisations where rules are needed to ensure that: the different needs of the pupils and staff are met; order is maintained; the school is kept as a safe environment; and a proper priority is given to teaching/learning. Children who have had disrupted childhoods will have experienced circumstances and situations that have been beyond their control. These will have left them with feelings of being insecure and vulnerable. They can react by displaying high levels of anxiety, fear of further rejection and uncertainty. These fears and anxieties can often be manifest in behaviours, which show little or no regard for rules and as difficulties in dealing with changes.

It will help your child if you can show that you know what the school rules are, and you support them. If your child understands that you know the rules and support them, and there are occasions when she/he feels that there has been an injustice or difficulties/conflict at school, then you need to talk this out at home. It is important to do so in a way which is quiet and calm, and which demonstrates your respect for the rules. Your self control is essential. When you are clear what your child thinks has happened, you need to get the view of school staff. Only then, can you play your part in finding a solution.

- **Try to meet, or at least learn the names of, your child's friends.**

At primary school, it is easier to meet other parents of children at the school, you are all likely to be local and so getting to know your child's friends is relatively easy. For younger children who are in the Looked After System or adopted, their histories, which may include a lack of continuity of care and schooling, can make it particularly difficult for them to make and sustain friendships. So doing what you can to promote friendships is very important. You might need to tailor the arrangements you make to the history and temperament of your child. So if your child finds it hard to share for example, you might start off making arrangements to take your child and a friend out to an activity like a playground or swimming or the cinema, rather than risk your child going into 'meltdown' when a friend visits the house and your child tries to protect precious toys! Making and keeping friends is a skill that needs to be learned, and supervised.

There will be more children in the secondary school than was the case in primary school. This offers much wider opportunities for your child to find a group of children who have similar interests. Often for many children, this is the beginning of establishing lasting friendships based on common interests. Your child will be making friends with children you have never met, because you are no longer taking your child to and from school each day and the catchment area for secondary school is much wider. If you can encourage them to bring their friends home and feel comfortable to do so, then this can help you to stay in touch with your child's social world.
Do try to learn the names of their friends. Staying in touch with your child's social world is important as one way of you monitoring their well-being. Changes in friendship groups or a sudden change in attitude to some named children, may be a first sign of difficulties with regard to bullying or loneliness. The most common consequence of peer rejection is aggression.

- **Keep a record of your child's timetable.**

    When children are at primary school, there are days when special equipment is needed: for swimming, or for a musical instrument lesson, or for football. You will greatly help your child if you can remember these and encourage your child to pack their own bag for school, and to include any special equipment that is needed for the day. It never really works to pack a bag at the last minute in the early morning rush. If children arrive at school without the things they need, it means they will feel disadvantaged, and they may be chided by the teacher. Children with disrupted childhoods and consequent low self esteem can overreact to being singled out.

    In secondary school, your child will be expected to bring equipment to school every day such as: pens, pencils, a ruler, textbooks for particular subjects, the right exercise books, ingredients for cooking, an overall for technology and a PE kit. As children get older, they need to develop skills of personal organisation with regard to this equipment. This is not an easy task for any child, and some children find it particularly difficult. Children, who have had difficulties in personal organisation and/or have had experiences of disruption at home or where home routines were never clearly established, find this particularly difficult. You can help your child with this if you have a copy of the timetable. You might want to adapt the timetable information into a list of equipment needed each day, and have that on your fridge or on the back of the door. In addition, having a copy of the timetable means you can monitor how you feel your child is settling in school. If you have a copy of the timetable and you notice your child has a particular reluctance to attend school on a certain day, you will be able to consider if it is related to the lessons on that day. Certainly the timetable would be a starting point for the discussion about a reluctance to attend school and/or change in mood/behaviour.

- **Establish and maintain a daily time when you can offer your child your undivided attention.**

    Regardless of the age of your child, establishing and maintaining a daily time when you offer your undivided attention is essential. When children are young, it seems obvious that you need to do this because they can't manage themselves and need close supervision.

    No matter how grown up and independent your child wants to be now, and especially when she/he has started at secondary school, she/he still needs your attention, care and support. It can be all too easy with your child's growing social independence, the demands of leisure activities, and homework, to find that days go by when you have both not found time to talk quietly to each other. This routine of having daily individual time is useful. On your part it signals the priority you place on listening to your child and taking an interest in what happens at school. It is a basis on which you can monitor your child's well-being. For your child, it is a predictable point in a busy day, when she/he can count on you and your interest. As children grow and face more of life's challenges, they still need to know that they are special. This is especially the case for children who are Looked After or adopted, whose sense of self esteem and security may be fragile. They need you to notice, value and praise their strengths, and to try to avoid blame. Blaming a child only confirms their low self esteem.

- **In the evenings, review the day and plan for the next day with your child.**

    A lot of children in the Looked After System or who are adopted, can be unsettled and volatile in their interactions with the outside world. They can lack knowledge about everyday situations and events, and lack the social skills to deal with these. They may need help to accept boundaries and the consequences of not managing to keep to them.

    It is part of the process of growing up, that we all make mistakes and need support when things don't go well. Using the daily one-to-one time and/or a routine of sharing news at a mealtime or at bedtime, can be a valuable way of helping your child. Checking out with your child demonstrates that you want to hear each day about what has gone well and what has been difficult, you are signalling your interest and your willingness to hear about the full range of their experiences. If you can establish with your child that you will listen to what has been difficult, try to see their point of view, talk with them about a range of solutions, involve them in choosing what to do next and not tell them what to do, then this will be invaluable. Children can learn as much, if not more, from making mistakes than they do from getting things right. What they need is non-judgemental adults, with whom they can share concerns and from whom they can get support when they need it. It is no use waiting until there is a difficulty before trying to establish yourself as a parent/carer who can listen and support. It is useful to have an established routine of reviewing the day in the evenings and planning for the next day, before difficulties arise.

- **Always attend arranged meetings, such as parents' evenings or individual option consultations or reviews.**

    There can be a lot of meetings arranged for parents/carers of children who are in the Looked After System. These can include:

    - The child's Looked After Review in which there will be discussions about school.
    - Personal Education Plan meetings/reviews.
    - If your child has special educational needs, there will be Termly Reviews/an Annual Review.
    - Parents' evenings which are for all parents/carers.
    - Special meetings about residential trips, subject options, examinations.

    These can be demanding on your time, especially if you have more than one child and/or you are in paid employment and you need to deal with your own work demands. Your child will know these meetings are planned and be part of a group of children discussing these in school. Children who have their own insecurities, anxieties and low self esteem, will appreciate (even if they don't show it) you demonstrating your commitment and involvement in their schooling.

    As parents/carers you will know about your child's earlier experiences and have thought about the messages the child may have taken from what has happened. You are special parents, who have been assessed and trained, and have ongoing professional support. You are therefore an important resource for your child's teachers. You can provide them with information and insights that they don't have, and which they need to manage and teach your child. Together you can demonstrate to your child, the benefits of adults working together.

    You will know about your child's history, strengths, difficulties, and the agencies working to support your family. The teachers who deal with your child need to have information to help them understand how best to teach and manage her/him. Parents/carers provide information when a child starts in a school. When children move to a new class, between Key Stages, from primary to secondary schools, or between schools, the parent/carer is best placed to check that key information/understandings are passed on between teachers/schools. Ask for an opportunity to meet your child's class teacher/form tutor at the start of each school year and check that information has been passed on. You can give your ideas of how your child is developing and what you see as her/his current needs.

- **When there are concerns, contact the teacher concerned and/or the form teacher as soon as you can.**

    Difficulties will arise. These could include a difficult lesson in which your child felt she/he didn't understand what was being taught, a problem with friends, lost books or equipment, bullying, or difficult behaviour which has resulted in sanctions being applied. Your child needs to feel that she/he can tell you her/his point of view. A child who has had a disrupted childhood and has experienced rejection, is likely to feel undeserving, and may be less able to explain to teachers what has happened at the time of the incident in school. So it is especially important that she/he feels understood at home. As a parent/carer, you need to bear in mind that there may be other points of view to be considered. Promptly contacting school and the right member of staff, will mean that you hear another point of view, have the opportunity to discuss what has happened, and be part of a positive solution to the difficulty. It is easier to deal with difficulties as they arise, as otherwise, what was a problem in one lesson with one teacher, can develop into a relationship problem for the teacher and the child, or a dislike of that subject which then affects your child's learning. Teachers will always appreciate it, if you contact them putting forward your understanding of what has been difficult, whilst signalling your willingness to hear another point of view and be part of a positive solution.

Here are the views of some young people in care, who are in Years 10 and 11 about what they feel has prevented them from getting on in school:

- Not getting clear communication from teachers to carers about how we are doing.

- Distractions from other students/often friends.

- Not having equipment, such as a computer and internet access, at home.

- The work being too hard.

- Teachers not taking the time to explain things when we don't understand it.

- Not having enough time to do homework.

- Being tired at school because we have to get up early to travel to school to be there on time.

- Being bored with lessons.

- **See yourself as a parent who nurtures if things go wrong.**

   It can be that the moves of placement for a child in the Looked After System or who has been adopted, don't coincide with the common entry points to school. Generally children share these common entry points: the start in reception class; the move to junior school; and transition to secondary school. Any change of school is difficult, but for a child moving to a new placement, the move of school can plunge the child into a school setting in a highly visible way. The child can feel like an intruder, and at worst be treated like one. Any lack of continuity in schooling will have undermined their progress, leaving them less able to make relationships with teachers and trust in their guidance. Mistrust acts as a barrier to the enjoyment of school and to educational success. Some children may have special educational needs which have not been identified because their earlier life militated against them being put forward for assessment, effective multi-agency liaison work, and a good understanding of their behaviours. Disruptions in school and care placements can lead to information being lost or interpreted differently by different adults. Unlike children who remain with their birth families, there may be no one person who can trace the child's history and have a view of her/his strengths and difficulties.

   Schools can be demanding places. Your child will make mistakes and difficulties will arise. As children grow older, and once they are at secondary school, parents/carers are less involved with school on a day-to-day basis. If you want to help your child face the challenges and difficulties that might arise, then you need to have signalled to your child beforehand that when things go wrong, that you will listen and you will nurture the child. Otherwise, your child will not tell you what happens at school and you will be less able to monitor her/his well-being and offer the support you would want to offer.

- **If your child has ongoing difficulties, then she/he may need additional daily support.**

   Children need to grow up knowing they have a secure place in a family, where their needs are met, where they learn about their rights and responsibilities in the family group, and on the basis of this they can explore, learn and become independent. It is on this basis that children learn to develop skills and competencies that are necessary for success in school. These include:

   - Secure self-esteem.
   - The capacity to manage feelings.
   - Accepting boundaries and rules in the classroom and in the playground.
   - Being able to wait, queue and take a turn.
   - Focussing on the task in hand and concentrating.
   - Being prepared to try difficult tasks and risk failure.
   - Accepting praise and criticism.

- Recognising the needs of others and the need to be helpful for the greater good.

These skills and competencies are necessary from very early on in education. It is worth considering how much more is expected of children and young people in secondary school. Children need to cope with:

- Expected independence from home, for example travelling unaccompanied over a greater distance.
- A much larger school setting.
- A much larger group of peers where instead of the child being one of the oldest, she/he is one of a group of the newest children, many of whom will unfamiliar to the child.
- As many as six changes of subjects, teachers, styles of teaching, and classroom settings each day.
- An increased volume of work and the need to organise subject specific resources/equipment, for example games kit, compass and ruler for Maths, dictionary for French, and so on.
- More independence of thought and work, evaluating what is taught and independent working on homework.
(see Chapter 8 on Secondary School transition for more details.)

All of this, is at a time of great personal upheaval which is adolescence.

For children in the Looked After System or who have been adopted and who have not had 'a warm, intimate and continuous relationship' and so are insecure, school can be a place where they underachieve, are seen as difficult, and where they either 'switch off or lash out. The challenge for teachers is to find ways to help them feel recognised and valued, to achieve their potential, and to develop emotionally and socially in a group setting. There are no simple solutions when difficulties arise. What follows are some guidelines that can be useful. In a secondary school, there would need to be a meeting of a child's subject teachers, to ensure all are aware of the child's difficulties and the guidelines for managing these.

- School staff need to be clear about the concerns for the child and how care plans are drawn up. **A key member of staff needs to attend Personal Education Plan (PEP) meetings** that are arranged to plan for your child's education.

- **Staff need to build in time, space, and a nurturing adult** to listen to your child, enable them to express their feelings, reduce anxiety, and when the time is right, reflect on their behaviour and discuss what has gone wrong, only then can there be planned joint strategies for coping.

- Establishing and maintaining **reliable, predictable routines** is helpful. Routines help the child to feel safe, they lower anxieties because what happens next is clear, and they reduce the likelihood that the child will over-react.

- While making mistakes is one way many children learn, for children who have been maltreated and who perceive the task in hand to be difficult, the likelihood is at best, they will be unwilling to try, and at worst, they will over-react, in ways which confirm their low self-esteem and distract everyone. Tasks set for the child need to be **appropriate to the child's age, stage, and abilities,** and set out in **finely-graded achievable steps.**

- Where a child knows that the teacher will **praise effort** as well as achievement, anxieties may be lower.

- Many may also need **specific help to get started, prompts for guidance, a clear view of what is expected, and praise given in a way which suits the child.**

- **Together with the teachers you may be able to anticipate vulnerable times** and provide planned support. Vulnerable times may be the start of the day, unstructured times such as breaks/lunch times, lessons the child finds difficult, transition and time between lessons.

- When the child is upset, overwhelmed, or difficult, it can be that remaining in the classroom is not the best option for the child or the other children or the teacher. School staff may need to **identify a safe place for the child,** where confrontation is less likely, where there can be safe supervision and nurturing.

- When the child needs a break from the tasks set or from the classroom, there needs to be resources for the child. **Concrete, rhythmic activities chosen with the child in mind, can provide a short-term distraction,** which allows all concerned to take time out. Activities can include: copying, colouring, decorating, doodle pads, music. It may be that you can give the staff ideas about what might best suit your child.

- It is important that all the staff dealing with the child find opportunities throughout the child's day to **provide positive noticing of the child's strengths and to seek to promote progress.**

- The challenge for the adults is to hold in mind, explanations for the behaviour of the child as well as providing appropriate responses to avoid triggering more anxiety and negative self-esteem. **It can also be that there are competing explanations for the child's difficulties which need to be assessed and provided for,** for example, a child who underachieves because she/he is dyslexic. The dyslexia complicates a history of poor care, abuse, and moves of family placement/schools.

- While the distress of children who have been maltreated is understandable, it doesn't mean that all teachers can cope with it all of the time. There needs to be **non-critical staff support** on which the staff can draw, for their personal and professional needs.

- Where systems already exist in school, a child may be helped by having **support from a buddy or peer mentor.** This can be a less anxiety provoking role model and may be a basis for learning to make social relationships.

- **It is helpful to organise regular reliable links between school and you as parents/carers** to ensure a positive working partnership on behalf of the child and to demonstrate to your child how adults can work together to prioritise education and the child's place in school. It may be better to have one named member of staff who deals with the contact, to avoid mixed messages.

- **Check that information about your child is reliably passed on a need to know basis.** Parent/carers provide information to a school when a child starts or moves schools. You know about the child's earlier experiences and have thought about the messages your child may have taken from what has happened. You are also more aware than most how your child is developing. When your child moves between classes, stages, primary and secondary, or schools, it is important that what is known is reliably passed on.

- **Find out about the range of support services that serve the school.**

  The Local Authority offers a range of support services to all schools. These are there to support the staff and the children, but they are also there to hear from you if you have particular concerns. Key services that you may need to contact are as follows:

  Behaviour Support Teacher ....

      Tel. No ....

      E-mail ....

  Educational Social Worker ....

      Tel. No ....

      E-mail ....

  School Nurse ....

      Tel. No ....

      E-mail ....

Educational Psychologist ....

　　Tel. No. ....

　　E-mail ....

School Counsellor ....

　　Tel. No ....

　　E-mail ....

Parent Governor ....

　　Tel. No ....

　　E-mail ....

Local Authority Education Officer ....

　　Tel. No. ....

　　E-mail ....

The Virtual School ....

　　Tel. No. ....

　　E-mail ....

For the children with special educational needs, there are additional specialist services and resources too numerous to list here. Check out with the school's Special Educational Needs Co-ordinator (SENCO), who will be able to tell you about more specialized help.

- **Talk to other parents/carers.**

Schools are busy complex places, which can leave parents/carers wondering where and how they fit in. There will be many occasions when you need information, advice and support. These might include:

  o When a child is newly placed with you and you are wondering about approaching a school for a place for the child.
  o When you want to find out about clubs and activities in the community to promote local friendships for your child.

- Children who are in the Looked After System or who have been adopted, may have difficulties in school whereby you feel you need ideas about what to do and how to get some support for yourself.

Other parents who use the school or are in Foster Carers/Adoptive parents' groups are a valuable resource for you. Having your own network of support is as important as support for your child. Talking to other parents can be an important first step.

- **Help your child have a rewarding and restful time out of school.**

  The children who do well in school are those who are supported at home and whose parents/carers are interested in their schooling. It is important that we as parents and carers, nurture the self esteem and social confidence of our children. It is on this basis that they will cope with challenges, deal with difficulties, and stay in touch with us.

Temper outbursts

I want to ask about the times when my eight year old daughter has had temper outbursts at home and in public. These seem to arise on occasions when either her dad or I ask her to do something that she doesn't want to do or we restate a boundary with regard to her behaviour. There are times when she can be defiant, rage in her anger and more rarely, kick and punch. We worry about these occasions as such outbursts are difficult to deal with, embarrassing in public, and a worry with regard to whether they might escalate in the future. An example would be when we go shopping in a supermarket. It always seems to start well with her helping me with our shopping list and finding items. It rarely ends well. She sees items she wants such as sweets or toys, and when I say she can't put them in the trolley, she can get very angry.

Adoptive Mum

Sit down with a cup of tea in a time of calm and review what you know about these outbursts. Talk to each other about how you feel when these outbursts happen and listen to each other, don't rush to criticise or give advice or find a fast solution. Try starting with a review of the problem by talking about:

- How often do these outbursts happen?
- Where do they happen?
- Who is there when they happen?
- What was going on before the outburst?
- What did you do during the outburst?
- What did you do after the outburst?

The answers to these questions will start you off on a path to managing better. Don't forget to see positives. If the outbursts are less frequent than you thought, or last for short periods of time, or don't happen in school, then take solace.

There needs to be consistency in the responses of both parents. If you make an observation that she is more likely to do this with one parent as opposed to another. Then you need to discuss this. It is not a given that the parent who is in charge when the outburst occurs, is mismanaging. It could well be the opposite. The parent who is not there may be giving in more, and this could underpin the outburst of rage from your daughter when the other parent sticks to her or his guns! This should lead you on to discuss a more consistent approach to that situation. While being firm and consistent with a little girl may at times be hard, it is useful to remember that little girls turn into adolescent girls!

Plan and prepare your daughter with clear expectations with regard to situations where outbursts have occurred in the past. For example when doing a supermarket shop, it might be useful to remind her as you go into the supermarket, 'we need to buy the things that are on this list, and I'm asking you to be helpful, perhaps we can take it in turns to find the items and put them in the trolley. When we have done the shop, we will deserve to have a drink in the cafe when you can choose a carton of drink of your choice.' This way she is given clear expectations, an example of how she can help, and a positive consequence if she does do so.

When any outburst occurs, unless the child's behaviour is life threatening or property wrecking, the best approach is to ignore inappropriate behaviour while keeping the child in sight and being mindful of the need to act. So if for example, your daughter begins to shout and rush off into a corner of the supermarket, it would be better to keep her in sight but to keep a distance and become preoccupied with checking the trolley or examining the receipts, and simply wait for her to calm down. Don't worry what other shoppers think. All of the shoppers who are parents, will have been faced with the same defiance in the past and are probably wishing you well, glad that this time it is not their problem. Even if other people don't understand, their opinion is not going to help you, so don't let yourself be troubled by what you imagine they are thinking.

When children do calm down after an outburst. it is really important that the focus of the adult is on moving on, not commenting on the outburst. Sticking with the supermarket example, when she stops shouting or chunnering in the corner, and comes towards you, the best thing is to focus forward and to say, 'well done, now we can finish the shopping and then go for a drink in the cafe'. It is really important to remember that when a child has lost their temper, that they are physically aroused, and it will be some time, in excess of 45 minutes before that level of physiological arousal subsides. In the meantime, it takes very little for them to start again, so it is in everybody's interests to remember this!

Ignoring outbursts is about modelling being calm. Children are much more likely to copy what we do, than to do what we say. It can help to remember that while the outburst feels to be personally directed at you, attempts to control the child only teach the child that bigger people control smaller people, and it is an inappropriate model. What we want is for our children to control themselves, and to know that we will see them doing this and praise them for it. It is in our power as parents to positively manage the situation by noticing and praising the ending of the outburst without reference to the difficult behaviours.

Asking a small child why they are having or have had a temper outburst rarely reveals any insights. The child is unlikely to understand why they have behaved like that and the question is only likely to: prompt them to feel ashamed, to worry about what to say; to fear the consequences of what they say; and perhaps, to say what they think the adult wants to hear. None of these will give you more insight. It is much better to say something along the lines of, 'I could see you were cross, but you did really well to calm down'. In this way the child's feelings are validated, but the adult restates the expectation and praises the child.

> **While outbursts are challenging for adults, it is essential to stay focussed on the positive.** When a child has an outburst and the adult is tired, we can find ourselves taxed by the situation. It will help you to remember that most children have temper outbursts, they are not personal even though you might be the target of their fury this time, they will pass, and that like most skills in life, learning to control one's temper takes time. Children learn quicker when adults remain focussed on positive expectations and manage to stay calm.

These ideas owe much to the book 'Behaviour Can Change' by E V S Westmacott and R J Cameron, published by Nelson Thornes Limited (1981). It is a very useful read.

8. That all important transition from primary to Secondary school

Introduction

When our children are very small, we chart their challenges and development in weeks and months. We all remember counting the weeks until that first magic smile or the months until they sit unaided or say their first words. In a child's early years, there are so many milestones and stages. We, as parents/carers, know we need to support our children to develop and learn new skills for themselves. As our children grow, the time between stages extends. The first day at school marks a huge step into the outside world for our children and for us. We prepare for it, discuss it and develop strategies to manage it for our children. It is clearly recognised as a challenge for children and their parents/carers. As our children develop physically, intellectually, emotionally and socially, becoming more independent, it can be the case that we underestimate the challenges presented for our child, by a move from primary to secondary school. This move is important educationally, but it can be a time of anxiety. This section of the handbook focuses on this transition point and in particular what parents/carers and children can tell us.

Understanding what the move from Primary to Secondary Education involves for your child

During a group for parents/carers, one of the mothers talked about the difficulties her child was having in school in Year 7. We started to talk about what the move from primary to secondary can mean for children. What follows are our ideas, which we hope will contribute to increasing the understanding of parents/carers.

- There is a huge change in the size of school from primary to secondary school.

- When children move to secondary school, children go from being in the oldest group of the biggest children in a small school, to being the youngest and smallest children in a large school.

- The number of subjects that the children study increase, which is interesting, and can be challenging.

- Students in secondary school have to be adaptable and meet very different teacher expectations in different subject lessons, for example drama makes different demands on children compared to the tight rules that are needed for chemistry in a laboratory.

- The different teachers for the different subjects will all have different personal styles and attitudes. The children need to understand these and adjust to them.

- A timetable of different subjects has the children moving round school for lessons. This can be confusing at first, and it also affects what children need to carry with them.

- The weight of school bags filled with books can be a health hazard for children who are still growing and developing.

- The transfer to secondary school usually means children have a greater distance to travel to and from school.

- Parents usually no longer walk with children to school, so the parents lose touch with the school/teachers and the friends/classmates of their child.

- For children, moving school usually means getting split up from friends and being put in different tutor groups. Some children find the prospect of new friends exciting, while others worry about this a lot.

- Secondary school years are the time of adolescence, which is a turbulent time for all young people.

- At this stage in children's development, there are huge peer pressures with regard to appearance, attitudes to work/teachers and friendships.

- There can be a sub-culture, which implies that it is 'naff' to accept awards and praise for work done. This can make it hard for children who want to work.

- Large schools need more rules than small primary schools. Some school rules can become the basis for conflict, for example how high are shoe heels, the colour/length of hair etc.

- Teenagers are much more aware of society pressures with regard to fashion, alcohol, smoking cigarettes, drugs, sex etc. Moving to secondary school opens children up to these pressures, as they see some older children challenging boundaries.

- At secondary school the playgrounds/fields are often extensive. These can provide space for activities like football, but they are also harder to supervise.

- There can be stories in the community about bullying, which make children nervous about going to secondary school. Stories such as being shoved in a locker or having your head put down the toilet.

- The way lunches are provided at secondary school is different from how they were provided at primary school. In primary school, food is often served to the children and they are closely supervised. In secondary school, lunches are usually served in a canteen style arrangement. Children need to learn to choose food, handle money or a payment card and decide where they want to sit. Some children find the numbers of children in the lunch hall and the queues difficult.

- There will be an arrangement for children getting free lunches. Some children can feel stigmatised by arrangements and it is important that the parents of children who get free meals, check out what the arrangements are for their child.

- The amount of homework increases.

- The levels of difficulties of homework also increase and it can be harder for the children to do and hard for the parents to help.

- There may be additional requirements of the school with regard to uniform and equipment/trips, which create pressures for parents financially.

(Prepared by Anne Peake with The Parents' Group, Springboard, Carterton).

What do children say about their worries?

One of the most important things you can do in the months before your child transfers to secondary school, is to talk to your child about the move, and **listen to what they have to say.** The class teacher in school will be talking about the move too. Most children have contact with staff from secondary school, perhaps a visit from their soon-to-be Head of Year and they have the opportunity to visit the school before the move. However, it is unlikely that your child will talk in school, in a class/group about the fears she/he might have. You can help your child by making time when you can talk about the move, when your talk can be uninterrupted and when you can give your undivided attention. It is a big move as we have already seen. There will be aspects of school that are eagerly anticipated, but there will also be fears. If you can encourage your child to talk about their worries, then you can get more information if it is needed, provide reassurance, and when necessary, ask for additional support from her/his class teacher and/or staff in the secondary school.

It is not always easy to begin a conversation with your child about her/his worries. In order to help you, we asked a group of children in two secondary schools just after they had joined the school, to write down the worries they had beforehand. You can look with your child at the range of comments the children made, and this might be a basis for you to ask, 'what worries do you have?' Altogether 90 children responded to a simple anonymous questionnaire.

There were some common themes to their answers to the question "what were the things you worried about most, before you moved to secondary school?" The four most frequently mentioned worries were:-

1	The size of the school and the problems of finding your way around it.	41/90 (45%)
2	The problem of bullies/bullying.	34/90 (37%)
3	Losing old friends and worrying about making new friends.	27/90 (30%)
4	Homework.	26/90 (29%).

What follows are the kinds of things the children said:-

What were the things you worried about most before you moved to secondary school?

- *I was worried about how I was going to get to school.*
- *Getting to school and lessons on time.*
- *That it will be a lot bigger.*
- *We were the highest in the school but now we're lowest.*
- *Being at the bottom of the school and in a massive school.*
- *Too many people.*
- *I thought I would get lost.*
- *Getting lost going from class to class.*
- *My friends finding new friends.*
- *Losing my old friends.*
- *Leaving my two best friends, one of which I knew from the first day of school.*
- *Friends because they go to different classes.*
- *Getting to know new people.*
- *Not making friends.*
- *I was worried about people picking on me.*
- *Being bullied by older people.*
- *What form I would be in.*
- *Bunsen burners in science.*
- *Teachers.*
- *Strict teachers.*
- *Too much homework.*
- *Forgetting books.*
- *I was worried about the homework and how organised you had to be, it is much more difficult than primary school.*

What is exciting about secondary school?

Children in the Looked After System or who have been adopted, have had experiences of change being thrust upon them, often in circumstances beyond their control. This can leave them with deep seated feelings of being insecure and vulnerable. So your child may be more anxious than her/his peers about the move to secondary school because of all the changes. It is therefore really important that you know about the opportunities that will open up for your child at secondary school. You can do a lot to help your child deal with this change by talking about the exciting features of secondary school.

- The opportunity to study a wider range of subjects in more depth.
- Specialist subject facilities such as a gymnasium, science laboratories, art and craft/design and technology facilities, the school library.
- Being in a bigger school with more pupils, means more opportunities to find friends with similar interests.
- Greater opportunities for sport, competitive games, and after school activities.
- More independence from home and from close supervision.
- It is a clear marker of a stage in growing up, thinking about a job/further education and being an adult.

What do children say they like most about being at secondary school?

As mentioned earlier, there are many aspects of secondary school that children eagerly anticipate. When talking about the move with your child, it would be helpful to talk about the positive opportunities and experiences that come with starting secondary school. Again, we learned so much from the children who responded to the questionnaire.

You can see that some of their worries, such as about friendships, rapidly became aspects that they liked most about being in secondary school. So while so many worried about the size of the school and getting lost, those same children talked about the school being bigger and the space there is, as features they now liked most. The four most frequently mentioned aspects the children liked were:

1.	The different subject lessons/clubs.	43/90	(48%).
2.	Friendships, especially making new friends.	33/90	(37%).
3.	Lunch arrangements/choices.	19/90	(21%).
4.	The size of the school and its resources.	17/90	(19%).

You can read with your child, the kinds of things the children said.

What do you like most about being in secondary school?

- All the different lessons.
- That you get to do better lessons and using new equipment.
- The classes and subjects are much better.
- You get different teachers for different subjects.
- Science because they have proper equipment.
- Lessons such as Art, Science and Maths.
- Most of the lessons like History.
- You get to learn French and German.
- P.E.
- The sports.
- When you go on the computers there are a lot more resources to use.
- Lighting the Bunsen burner.
- In primary school there was nothing good and I like woodwork and they did not do that.
- You do proper lessons.
- Moving around for each lesson.
- My form tutor.
- Brand new teachers, equipment, start.
- Having the library.
- So many new people.
- Getting to know more people that you never knew before.
- All my new friends.
- Break.
- Bringing a football in because we could not before.
- The canteen is very nice.
- The food.
- It's bigger better lunch.
- You get to choose more freely what you want for lunch.
- You can eat outside.
- The space.
- It's very big you can get lost sometimes.
- It's a challenge.
- I like Wednesdays best, because you get to leave at 2.00pm
- Lots more clubs like drama, hockey, juggling and trampolining.
- Lockers.
- Getting a bit more care.
- Getting more responsibility.
- Being big and grown-up.

Support for children to manage the transition

This move from primary to secondary school is difficult and exciting. It can feel like everything is about to change, and for children who are in the Looked After System or who have been adopted, changes can be deeply unsettling. This is a time when your reassurance and encouragement is most needed.
School staff are aware of the need to support children as a group and individually. All primary schools co-operate with their secondary school to do what they can to support children to make this move. Ideas vary about how best to do this. If you feel your child is going to need extra help it would be useful to start to discuss this early on in Year 6. If your child is in the Looked After System, you could raise your concerns at the first PEP review in Year 6. If your child is adopted, ask the school SENCo about the types of support that will be available. Here is an outline of the kinds of support that can be offered.

Different schools offer different support.

- **Year 6 Transfer Meetings.** These are professional meetings where teachers/SENCOs from primary schools meet the Head of Year 7/ SENCO/Form Tutors from the secondary school and discuss children about whom there are concerns. The meeting might highlight the support a child needs such as: a named TA, to be in a class with a known friend, extra help with maths or personal organisation.

- **Year 6 classes visit the secondary school.** All schools organise Year 6 pupil visits. Often the visits involve allowing the children to use some of the special resources such as: the sport facilities, a climbing wall, science laboratories and drama studios. These give the children enticing glimpses of what is exciting about secondary school.

- **The primary school may have an 'ambassador' system.** This is where the class of Year 6 pupils discuss the move and make a list of questions they have. The teacher then arranges for a small group of children with a supporter to visit the secondary school and get some answers, bringing these back to the class. Skilfully used, this can be a way of giving status to the child(ren) ambassadors, building confidence, if it is needed.

- **Teachers from secondary schools teaching lessons in primary schools prior to transfer.** This is an interesting way to help pupils think about the transition. Secondary school teachers may come to the primary school to show how lessons are delivered, this shows them changes while they are still in primary school. They can discuss these afterwards with familiar teachers.

- **Individual children visiting a secondary school.** Some children are not able to cope with a visit when they are part of a large group. This may be because they have significant learning difficulties, or are physically or socially very frail. Options then can include visiting with a group, but with one-to-one support, visiting on their own with a supporter and taking digital pictures to enhance work done with them about the transition.

- **Guided work about the transition.** There are materials written to help parents and children to plan for secondary school transition. The 'Moving On' parents' handbook and child's colouring book are an example. The colouring book sets a series of tasks for the child which are easy to do, but which highlight features of secondary schools, such as: the expectations about wearing uniform, reading a timetable, choosing a meal in the school canteen, thinking about different subjects and learning who is there to help.

- **Specific interventions to support a child prior to transfer.** Some children have been identified at primary school as needing input from Education support agencies such as the Behaviour Support Service or the Educational Psychology Service. When these professionals are already involved, they may well make a planned intervention to help an individual child prior to transfer, for example working on anger management sessions with a child who has behaviour difficulties.

- **The allocation of a named supporter.** Where a child is thought to have significant difficulties, which may adversely affect the child's capacity to cope, discussions can be had with support staff in the secondary school. It may be that having a named supporter is helpful. Sometimes, a weekly one-to-one with a supporter can be useful to iron out organisation problems, or friendship issues, or recording homework tasks, or project deadlines.

- **For some children, there will be special arrangements which need to be in place before transfer.** There will be children who have very individual special needs and for whom there need to be special arrangements made in advance. An example of this is an arrangement made for a child with cerebral palsy, to have two lockers at a height that suits her, to accommodate her equipment and to avoid her needing to carry too much at any one time.

- **Nurture groups for Year 7 students.** Many schools build in support for children as they start secondary school. For example, one school plans the Year 7 timetable for the whole intake, to minimise the number of staff changes between lessons and moves between rooms for all year 7 pupils. Another school runs a weekly group for more vulnerable children where they can meet, talk over any concerns they have, and be guided by a concerned member of staff.

- **Planned involvement of Education Support professionals after transfer.** It may be that the primary school teacher feels that a child may find transfer difficult, but wants to wait to see how she/he manages the transition. The fact that the child is moving with their class group means she/he has the support of peers. They will learn from each other and most children grow with the experience, as the survey at the start of this section shows. All schools have input from Education Support agencies and can call on their support when there are particular concerns.

The transition from primary to secondary school is a big step for children. If you are worried, talk with the primary school staff and they will help you and your child. Remember that most children manage well and are justifiably proud of themselves.

School Files

My daughter is due to transfer to secondary school next year. I knew the teachers in her primary school well and they knew she is adopted, and they have learned to deal with her well. When I talked to her about moving school, she said that she doesn't want all the teachers in her new school to be told she is adopted. She feels this can lead to her being seen differently and she wants to be the same as everyone else. I understand this, but I can't help worrying about her. I feel that it would be best if there was someone in school who did know she is adopted, and that she can be quite insecure and anxious if she feels under pressure. What do schools put in children's files? Will it be in her file that she is adopted? Does her file move with her? If I did want to tell a member of staff in school, who would you suggest that I tell?

Adoptive Mum

All transition points in school are times when parents and children can become anxious about change. Moving from primary to secondary school is a significant transition point for all children. In particular, it can be very worrying for children who have had disrupted childhoods. It may be that your daughter's desire to be the same as everyone else is part of her way of dealing with her worries about change.

Here are some ideas in response to your question:

- Make sure that you talk to her about all the positive opportunities she will have when she moves school.

- Have a look in the last section at what children have said about their fears about the moving to secondary school. Use this as a basis for helping her to talk about what she fears, and together discuss dealing with these.

- Find out from her primary school teacher/Headteacher what the secondary schools already do to ease the transition. If you feel she needs extra support, you should discuss this with her teacher and ask for advice.

- Schools do keep individual files for children. Parents/carers have the right to ask to see their child's file.

- School files on children contain:
    - Records of progress.
    - Copies of school reports.
    - Notes of meetings with parents.
    - Information about a child's special educational needs if this is relevant. (The class teacher and SENCO will also have this information).

    You will find that you have already seen what is in the file in your day-to-day dealings with the school.

    The files do not contain confidential information such as Safeguarding paperwork. All schools hold these records separate from the child's file, in locked drawers, and with the access to them being carefully restricted.

- There may be a reference in the file to the fact that she was adopted by your family. Ask the Headteacher of her primary school to discuss this with you. One way to have a reference to her adoption in the file, in a way, which helps teachers, would be to ask if the leaflet 'The Adopted Child in School' could be included in the file.

- The files do move from primary to secondary school when the children move. Before they are moved, they are checked and any out of date information that will not be needed, is removed.

- If you do want to tell someone in school that she is adopted, you could consider telling one of the following:
    - Her Head of Year
    - The Designated Teacher for Children who are Looked After
    - The Special Educational Needs Co-ordinator
    - The School Counsellor (if there is one).

    Your child will need to know who knows, if she does need someone to talk to or some extra help, she can approach the person **who knows.**

9. Support for children doing homework

Introduction

When children are provided with homework by their school, it can be as much of a challenge to the parents/carers, as it is to the children. Homework is a regular feature of all secondary schools and an increasing feature of work in primary schools. What is clear is that supporting children to do homework is not a simple process and many parent/carers would benefit from advice and support about this. This is intended to provide some basic ideas for parent/carers. If as a parent/carer reading this, you have a need for more advice, then do get in touch with staff in your child's school. If your child is in primary school, then it is best in the first instance to talk to the class teacher. If your child is in secondary school, then you could approach the subject teacher who has set the homework if the problem is specific, or the form tutor, or the Head of Year.

Before making specific plans to support your child doing homework, it is useful if you begin by thinking about the style of preparation and organization that the child has seen previously in their family of origin. The style that parents/carers have in dealing with their preparations for their work/special events, is likely to be the most powerful influence on how their children prepare for their schoolwork/school day. For many children in the Looked After System, their early experiences have been ones of disadvantages, and at worst abuse. They may well have had few positive experiences of parent figures supporting them in school.

Now the children are in the Looked After System or adopted, parents/ carers need to think about the models they provide, which can help/not help the child concerned. At the risk of labouring the point you should also think about your styles as parents/carers with regard to personal organisation. If getting up for work for you means, getting up late, dashing around the house feverishly looking for your car keys, wondering where your work diary is; or if you don't work, getting the children up for school is a hasty, disorganized and hectic process as you try to find the PE kit for the day, only to find it is muddy and unwashed in a corner; then you really do need to consider the messages you are giving your child/children about preparation and organization. If you want them to be successful at school and you want to support them with their homework, then it might be that you need to change too. If you are sharing the parenting of your child/children with a partner, then you might want to think together about the messages that your children are receiving, about the way in which different genders approach the need for preparation and organization, with regard to work and special events.

The Aim of Homework

Homework will play an increasing part in your child's education as she/he grows older. It helps if you are clear about the aims of homework in your child's education. If you can discuss these aims with your child/children, they are more likely to be able to approach homework set for them by the school in a positive manner. The aims of homework are:

- It can extend the work that the children have done at school.

- It provides a basis for teachers to check if a child has understood the work that has been done at school, and can demonstrate this in work without the support of the teacher and classmates.

- It is a means of showing children that they can achieve work done independently.

- It offers an opportunity for children to work at their own pace, and for some children to demonstrate a particular interest in a subject.

- It is useful for you as parents/carers to be able to see the work that your child is doing in school and it can be a basis for offering individual attention and praise to your child for achievements in school.

- Supporting your child with her/his homework is providing you with an opportunity to be an active partner in your child's learning, and maybe to learn something yourself.

Tools of the Trade

Just like any job that is worth doing, you need the right 'tools of the trade' for doing homework. As any teacher knows, a major starting point for getting any work done, is the battle to ensure that everyone has the things that they need to do the task being set. Once your child is doing homework, then that battle will rage in your house too. It will be useful if you can organize for there to be a box or drawer in your house which has the resources, which are usually needed for doing homework.

These resources can include:
- pens
- pencils
- colouring pencils/felt tips
- pencil sharpener
- rubber
- ruler
- glue
- scissors
- a compass
- correction fluid
- possibly a calculator
- if possible, access to a computer

Setting the Scene for Homework

If you are caring for young children who are too young for school or are not yet being set homework, it can help them if you encourage habits of quiet time, for reading and drawing. This will be a helpful basis for moving to doing homework later.

If the school your child attends, is setting homework, then you can be assured that there will be a system to this. In order to help you understand the homework system you could:

- Ensure that you and your child know what the homework system is. At primary school, the class teacher will have regular days when homework is set and most secondary schools have set homework timetables for children.

- Make sure you have your own copy of the school planner/homework diary and a spare copy for when your child loses hers/his.

- It might be useful if you have a notice board in your kitchen, then you can keep a copy of the homework timetable on that.

- Older children may be working on projects which require extended work over days/weeks, it can help to have a long-term planner on which you can note, when projects are set and when they are due to be handed in.

- Most important of all, is to set aside time each evening when you and your child talk about the work that has been set by the school.

If you have the room for flexibility, then you may need to talk as a family, about arranging a setting in which your children can do their homework. It is important that any setting, which your child is going to regularly use to do their homework, has the possibility of a work atmosphere. The setting needs to have the following features:

- A work surface for the child.
- A chair on which to sit.
- The possibility of quiet.
- Away from the distractions of the television.
- Some children are helped by background music, this will vary with the task set.

If you have more than one child with homework then setting the scene becomes more complicated. You will need to consider:

- Whether your children work together or separately.
- Whether the children work at the same time or different times.

Offering Help

It will be helpful if you begin by discussing with your child, the times when they will do homework. If your child feels that she/he has been involved in making decisions about when homework is done, then it's more likely that it will be done. Ideas for timing include:

- **Most important of all, negotiate the time when homework will be done in relationship to the child's preferred activities.** For example, it is no use insisting that homework is done as soon as your child comes home from school, if she/he is tired and hungry, and plainly needs a break. Nor are you likely to be popular or get the homework done, if you insist it is done at the time of their favourite television programme, or at the moment they choose to go out with a friend. It needs to be said, that it will not work just leaving it to your child to make the decision. One of the essential features of being a child, and one of the joys, is to live in the present and not to want to think and plan for tomorrow. So negotiate a time, which suits your child and your family.

- **If there is more than one piece of homework to complete in a given evening/weekend, it can be helpful to discuss with your child the order in which pieces of work are done.** It is rarely successful to leave a difficult and taxing piece of work to be the last piece of work to be completed, when the child has become tired and it is getting late. It is often best to do the most difficult and complex work first, and then to do the less demanding pieces when the child is more tired. These might include drawing or copying or mounting work.

- **You can better support your child, if you are clear about how long children are expected to spend on their homework; schools usually have guidelines about this.** You can then keep an eye on how much time they are spending on work, with a view to making sure that they don't work too hard or for too long. If it is the case that they are spending far more than is expected of them on the piece of work, then you can make a parent/carer's decision about when they are too tired, and if need be slip a note or a post-it sticker into their homework book, explaining why they have stopped at the point that they have.

- For older children with more pieces of work to do, some of which may have extended deadlines, **you may have to help your child prioritise which pieces of work need to be done when.**

- **Many secondary schools encourage children to have a 'study buddy',** this is another child with whom they can check out when they are not sure what to do. It is a great help if they have the telephone number of someone in their class/subject group who is reliable and whom they can telephone, when they are not sure.

You need to consider how you will use your presence to support your child when she/he is doing the homework. Your decision about this will be influenced by your child's abilities/confidence about a piece of work, your child's temperament, your child's wishes, and maybe your own abilities/confidence in the subject. Options for how you will use your presence can include:

- Being with them as they start their work.
- Sitting with them as they do the work.
- Being there when the work is finished to help them check and acknowledge the efforts they've made.
- Keeping an eye on the way your child uses the computer for homework. Time spent on surfing the net or chat rooms, can be very distracting.
- Being positive, and praising your child for trying. If they make mistakes, it is better to make comments such as 'nearly', rather than 'wrong', and encourage them to try again.
- Above all, be encouraging and supportive, and not overwhelming.
- Remember that the homework is for the child to do, not you!

When starting to do a piece of work it is helpful if you can encourage your child to think about the work before he/she starts. Things to think about are:

- What is the piece of work that has been set?
- Why has this piece of work been requested?
- What is the teacher asking for in setting this piece of work?

If you and your child agree you are sitting with them as they work, just before the child begins a piece of work, you can help with prompts such as:

- Reminding your child about the need for a date, title and margin for the work, and the need to lay out work in a way, which does justice to it.

- Discuss the way that they are going to order their ideas.

- Encourage your child to use scrap paper to plan work where appropriate.

- If you feel confident discuss the content of the work.

When the homework involves learning for a test, these basic ideas might be useful:

- There is no substitute for working on your own in a quiet place, reading and re-reading work you need to learn. A lot depends on the work that needs to be learned, but it may be possible for your child to read the work out loud, making a recording of what they have to learn. They can then replay this in their bedrooms, and/or on an ipod as they walk to school, or in the car as they travel.

- Having a summary sheet of key points can sometimes be a useful aid to learning.

- It is a great help when children have to learn things for school, if parent/carers can make time to offer to test them on what they have learned.

Follow-up

The extent that you are able to follow-up on work that your children have done for homework is a further way that you can support them in school. They will be more encouraged if you express a clear interest in how the work was marked. It is really important not just to focus on the marks, but to be asking questions about what the teacher's comments were about the work and any ideas that the child/teacher had about how the work could be improved.
Always remember to praise your child for the efforts that they made, and never judge your child against classmates, or brothers and sisters. The only way to make judgements about how well a child has done, is to make comparisons with work done previously, and to encourage children to do their personal best.

Points to Remember

1. **Do make sure that your child has time every evening and at points during the weekend for fun and relaxation, and when you as a parent/carer can nurture them.** You will not help your child to be happy and achieve at school, if they don't have time off on a regular basis.

2. It will be helpful to you and your child if you **can establish a pattern of positive contacts with the staff in your child's school,** rather than developing a pattern of contact with the school in a crisis. It will help you if you can know the structure of your child's school:

    for primary schools this usually includes:
    the Headteacher
    the class teacher
    the Special Educational Needs Co-ordinator

    for secondary schools this includes:
    the form tutor
    the names of subject teachers
    the name of the Head of Year
    the SpecialEducational Needs Co-ordinator
    Head of Lower/Middle School/Sixth Form

3. **Many secondary schools offer a homework club.** It would be useful to find out what this entails, and whether it is suitable for your child and the work that she/he needs to do.

4. **Check out what library facilities the school has,** the times when the library is open, and the extent to which you and your child can draw on these resources, should the need arise for homework.

5. **Check if the school provides additional resources.** The school may have a facility for buying stationery, second-hand books, and software, which might be useful for your child.

6. **Check out with the school, if there are times after school, when your child can use the computer/word processor facilities.** Ask if there will be support and supervision to use these.

Just as it was suggested earlier that you encourage your child to have a 'study buddy', it can be helpful for you to be part of a network of parents/carers with whom you can discuss homework in general, particular pieces of work, and get support for yourself in the very difficult task of supporting children to do homework.

Above all remember that your job as a parent/carer is to support your child and that you will do this most effectively by providing them with good examples of preparation and organization yourself. Involve them in the way you support them, be positive in the way you support them, and remember that you are their parent/carer and not their teacher.

(Notes on homework prepared by Anne Peake and Rosemary Trace)

Behaviour problems in school

R is 12 years old. She has been living with us for four years. She loved her primary school, but problems have arisen since she transferred to secondary school. She has begun to mix with what I would say is 'the wrong crowd', but who she thinks are her friends. She has started to be rude to teachers, being disruptive in class, walking out of class, and not doing homework. I am really worried about it all.

Foster Mum

I can understand how worried you must be. As was said in the section on supporting children in school, it is important she feels understood at home. At the same time, you need to be contacting school to hear their views about what is happening, so you can be involved in the discussions and a part of the ideas for strategies to help her. The following points are worth bearing in mind:

- All schools have structures of staff responsibilities to help individual children who present difficulties. These include: form tutor, Head of Year, a senior member of staff with responsibilities for pastoral care, the Special Educational Needs Co-ordinator, the Counsellor, and the Designated Teacher for Children who are Looked After. Parents/carers should clarify who is dealing with the problems in school and talk to that member of staff.

- All schools have policies with regard to managing behaviour and with regard to bullying. These are usually available on the school website and/or you can ask for a copy of these.

- All schools have regular input from named professionals in school support services, such as the Educational Psychology Service (EPS). Where schools have particular difficulties dealing with a young person with regard to attendance, behaviour, or learning, then teachers can identify professionals who can be called in to support the school staff, and add to what the school has already done.

- Where children who are in the Looked After System or who have been adopted, have problems, over and above what can usually be dealt with by the school and its support agencies, the Virtual School will have staff who can help.

- Sometimes, it is felt that a short period of time out of school might be useful to allow all concerned to have some time to reflect. Read the section on the question about exclusions.

- When it is felt that the difficulties are such that the child would benefit from 'a fresh start', the school and/or the parents/carers should contact the Education Officer for the school to get their advice and support with the process. SEN Officers deal with children who have an Education Health and Care Plan (EHCP) and Inclusion Officers deal with the other children.

10. Managing your child's use of computers and the internet

Schools have computers and the use of the internet, as integral resources in the education process. Uses include: researching information, learning about how to effectively present information, storing and networking information, communicating in school and between schools and with the wider community.

Schools have systems, which enable school staff to monitor e-safety, with a view to ensuring children use ICT in school in a safe way, stay on-task during lessons, and act responsibly online. The school will have a policy/code of conduct with regard to the use of computers and the internet, and you will have been sent a copy of this. Both you and your child will have been asked to sign your agreement to the code of conduct. This code will apply at all times, in and out of school hours, whilst using school equipment. It will also apply to misuse of home computers and mobile phones to bully or threaten other pupils. Here is an example of such a code of conduct:

You should:

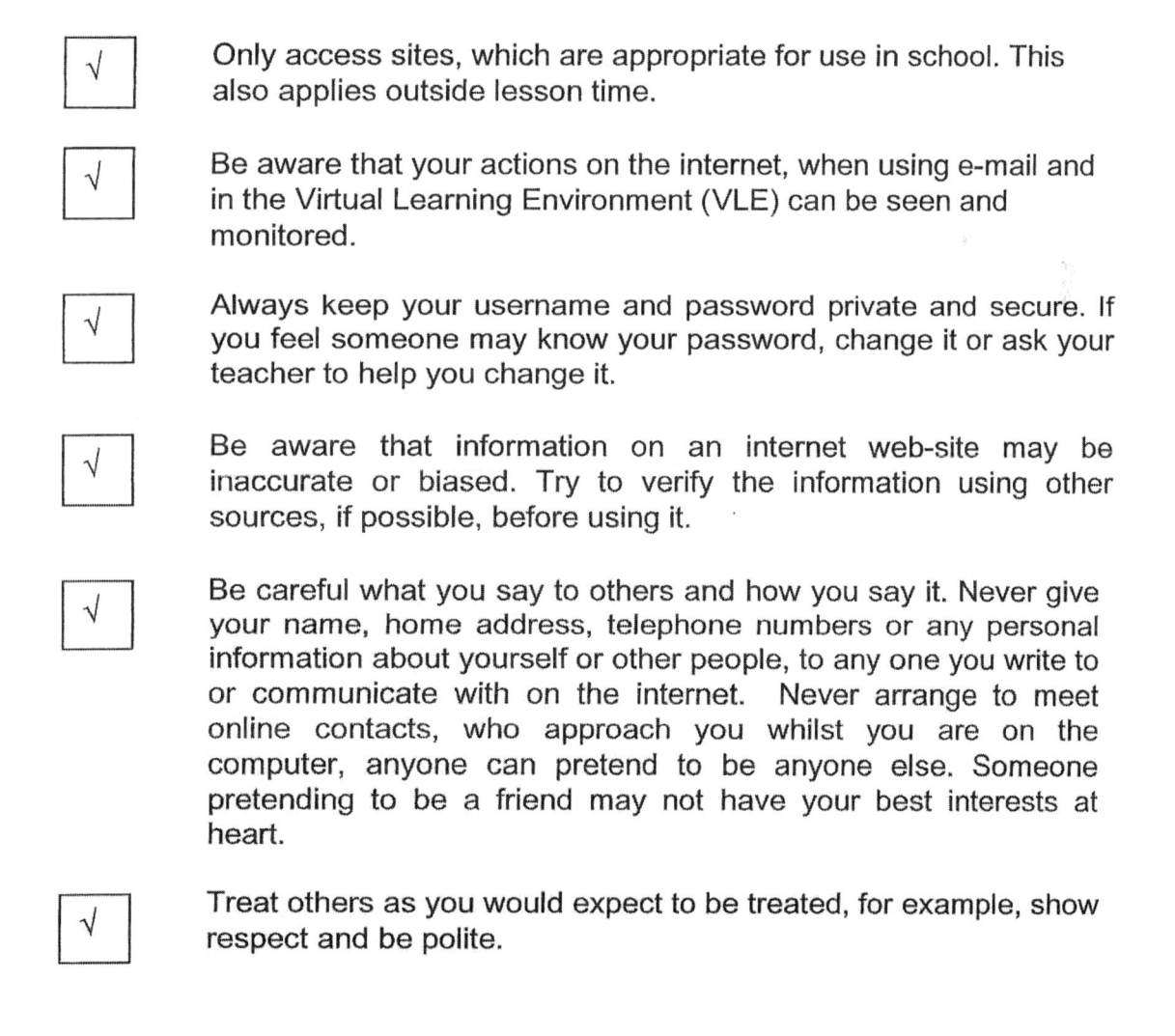

- [√] Only access sites, which are appropriate for use in school. This also applies outside lesson time.

- [√] Be aware that your actions on the internet, when using e-mail and in the Virtual Learning Environment (VLE) can be seen and monitored.

- [√] Always keep your username and password private and secure. If you feel someone may know your password, change it or ask your teacher to help you change it.

- [√] Be aware that information on an internet web-site may be inaccurate or biased. Try to verify the information using other sources, if possible, before using it.

- [√] Be careful what you say to others and how you say it. Never give your name, home address, telephone numbers or any personal information about yourself or other people, to any one you write to or communicate with on the internet. Never arrange to meet online contacts, who approach you whilst you are on the computer, anyone can pretend to be anyone else. Someone pretending to be a friend may not have your best interests at heart.

- [√] Treat others as you would expect to be treated, for example, show respect and be polite.

√	Always tell your teacher or another adult if you ever see, hear or read anything, which makes you feel uncomfortable whilst using the internet, e-mail or VLE.
√	Respect copyright and trademarks. You cannot use the words or pictures that you see on an internet site without giving credit to the person that produced the information originally. You must not copy text or pictures from the internet and hand it in to your teacher as your own work.
√	Check with a teacher before downloading files, or completing questionnaires, or subscription forms, or opening e-mail attachments.

You should not:

X	Send, access, store or display offensive messages or pictures.
X	Use or send bad, threatening or annoying language, nor any language, which might incite hatred against any ethnic, religious or other minority.
X	Access any other user's files, e-mail, or personal webspace, without their express permission.
X	Intentionally waste resources.

Please note:

You should always log out and close your browser, when your session has finished.

User areas on the school network will be closely monitored and staff may review your files and communications to maintain system integrity.

Failure to follow the school code will result in the loss of your access to it. Further disciplinary action may be taken if appropriate. If applicable, external agencies may be involved as certain activities may constitute a criminal offence.

Your child's use of computers and the internet will be monitored very closely in school.

The difficulties that might arise, are more likely to occur out of school when children use home computers, with hand-held electronic devices or smart phones, belonging either to your child or to friends.

Computers and the internet are the darlings of today. Anyone who doesn't agree, risks being deemed to be technologically incompetent or paranoid. Yet, we know that the misuse of computers and the internet can be dangerous for children and young people. Some children and young people are especially vulnerable; children who are disabled/have special needs, children who are in the Looked After System or have been adopted, and children who have histories of being neglected or abused.

Guidelines for parents/carers

Parents and carers should be aware of basic guidelines, which may reduce the risks of misuse of computers and the internet, in their home. Ideas for these are:

- **Check your computer facilities.** If you are buying a computer for family use or you want to review the system you have, seek advice from reputable retailers with regard to what internet safety devices they would recommend to restrict child access to inappropriate material. Software is available to filter inappropriate sites. When young people are using computers in friends' houses, at school, or in the library, the safety devices may be different. Discuss this with the young person.

- **Learn about the computer yourself,** understand how you can access a record of the history of use on the computer, and then periodically use this facility. If, as one carer reported, you have a young person who is able to wipe this record clean, then you may need to have to insist that the history function on the computer is not wiped clean, or access to the computer will be denied.

> *I asked her what site she was on and she told me the name. It sounded like a children's site name and I was reassured. When I looked at what they were talking about, it was all about sex, including the rape of a 12 year old girl. I was really shocked. I didn't know how to check up on the history of use before, but I do now.*
>
> *Foster Mother*

- **Place the computer in a living-room.** It is easier to monitor the use of the internet, if the computer which has internet access, is placed in a communal room in the home. The adults are more likely to see what is on the screen, at times which can't be predicted by the young person. Paedophiles have said, with regard to computers which have web cams, that if they can see that the computer is in a communal room, then that is a restraining factor for them with regard to contact with the young person using the computer.

- **Talk about computer use.** Children and young people need help to enjoy the internet and make positive use of it. It can help them if parents/carers are able and willing to talk about how they use the internet, in much the same way as parents/carers talk to children and young people about books they have read or films they have seen.

- **Set limits to time spent on the computer.** In encouraging our children to manage computers and the internet, it is important to recognise that this is not a substitution for real social contact and other activities. Limiting time that a young person spends on the computer is a helpful boundary to set. Children need to be encouraged to enjoy other activities: playing with friends, family activities, hobbies, sports etc.

> *When I talked to my friend, I found out that she limits the time her children can spend on the computer to half an hour in the evening. I feel I should have done that, rather than wait till it got out of hand with him spending hours on the computer in his bedroom and not wanting to do anything else.*
>
> *Foster Mother*

- **Manage the information from the internet.** When they are using the computer and accessing the internet, children need teaching how to manage the information they find. Without support, children and young people are likely to think that because the information is on the internet, it is right and to be believed.

- **Young people need training to learn to not give out personal information over the internet.** They should not give out information about their name, their address, their date of birth, their telephone number or their school. If the activity is such that they feel they need to identify themselves, then they should use a nickname, but not one which identifies their age or has sexual connotations.

> *Sometimes I look at the names of her friends on their email accounts and I worry about what it all means and the messages they are giving to people, like sexyknickers@...........*
>
> *Mother*

- **Guard the personal information of others.** It is also important that they learn not to give out this same information about family members or friends.

- **It is important to teach young people that the people they 'meet' online, are not 'friends', and they might not be who they say they are.** It can be useful to have a discussion with a young person about how we judge people to be friends. A friend is someone that we know, with whom we have a mutual relationship of trust and understanding, and where the relationship is mutually supportive. It can help young people if adults are clear with their language, referring to people children meet online as an 'online contact' or a 'computer pal' (rather like a pen pal). In this way parents/carers are signalling by their language, a distinction between a friend and someone met online.

- **The dangers of meeting up with people from online contacts.** Young people need to be warned of the dangers of meeting up with people with whom they have been in contact online, regardless of what the person says. It is helpful to young people to set the boundary of not arranging to meet someone without talking to parents/carers first and never going alone to meet a person with whom they have had contact online.

> My 14 year old was on a site called 'Wicked Colours' for teenagers. It seemed okay, until she said to me 'What's our telephone number', and when I asked her why she was asking, she said that she was going to meet someone she'd met online, in Oxford.
>
> I asked a teacher to check the site, and he found pop-ups, which were literally soft pornography. I was really worried because she'd taught my eight year old grandchild how to find the site.
>
> *Foster Mother*

- **Learn about social network sites and chat rooms.** Parents/ carers need to understand what social network sites, chat rooms and instant messaging, are, and to be clear which are monitored and which are open. Parents/carers should learn how privacy levels can be set up on social networking sites, and show the young person how to protect themselves. Again, consulting a reputable retailer can provide parents/carers with information about software packages, which can be used to switch off a computer when inappropriate language is used. This means that when a young person is using the internet, and loudly complains that the computer has "crashed", it will alert a supervising adult to the possibility that inappropriate talk/material has been accessed.

- **Know about the use your young person makes of social network sites.** If parents/carers know that a young person is using a social network site, it might be useful to consider insisting on seeing a sample of the photographs and/or messages on the site from time to time. Few young people, especially teenagers, will agree to all the material they have put on the site being scrutinised all the time. However, a random check and the reaction this produces, might alert an adult to the possibility that misuse is occurring. Young people posting suggestive pictures or videos of themselves, are putting themselves at risk. The capacity of abusing adults to overcome what young people think are safeguards on these sites should never be underestimated.

> *My daughter was on Bebo when a message came out of the blue, it was from a man in America and it had a photograph of him dressed in a tuxedo. In the message he said that his wife had died and he was worried because his daughter was having problems with her periods and he was asking if he could talk to my daughter about this ...... I pressed the reply button and typed in 'pervert' and sent it back.*
>
> *Adoptive Mother*

If something like the above happens to you or your child, the Child Exploitation and Online Protection Centre, CEOP, recommend not replying, blocking the message, and then reporting the incident by clicking on the 'report abuse' button that exists on many networking sites.

- **Chain e-mails,** purporting to be in support of a needy group, or to bring good luck, or a threat if the conditions are not complied with, can be passed between groups of children/young people and their acquaintances. If this happens, the addresses on the chain e-mail can provide an abuser with a list of contact email addresses, which can then be misused. Reporting potential abuse through e-mails such as these is recommended, as is saving the e-mails as evidence.

> *My daughter got a chain e-mail from a school friend. It said she had to send it to ten friends or something bad would happen to her. It said someone would come into her bedroom at night and kill her. It had a picture of what was said to be a dead girl. She was really upset that anyone should send it to her and so was I. When I thought about it, I thought that the pages and pages of email addresses were likely to be girls like her and would be a gift of contact addresses for a paedophile. So I telephoned the Police and they took the e-mail.*
>
> *Mother*

- **Be reassuring.** Parents/carers need to reassure young people, that if they have done or said things or are uncomfortable with their use of the internet, that we all make mistakes. As a parent/carer, you can make it clear that you see your job as to help them when they make mistakes. It is important that young people are not more fearful of the supervising adults, than they are of what they might encounter on the internet.

- **If a young person has downloaded pornography,** then it is important that the parent/carer restricts their use of the internet and consults with professionals about this. Questions need to be asked about from whom, how, and when has the young person learned to do this? The young person might need support from suitably qualified and experienced professionals whose work is with regard to assessing and treating young people with sexual behaviour problems. Parents/carers also need to consult about the fact that the material has been accessed on the internet and downloaded onto their machine. This may mean having a discussion with the Police. It could well be that the access that has been made to a site offering pornography, could be identified later in a Police investigation. So it is important to discuss your concerns as soon as possible, and check if the machine needs to have the material cleared from it.

- **Be in charge.** Above all, parents/carers should remember that they are in charge of young people who use computers to access the internet in their homes. If misuse is suspected, then the parent/carer should investigate locking devices, which prevent internet access at times when there are no supervising adults, or while they discuss the misuse with the young person. A fuse or a computer lead can be removed to stop all use, if need be. Children do need to access the internet for school work, so parents/carers need to ensure they can do so in supervised safe settings.

> *I only let my children on the computer that doesn't have internet connections. That way, I don't worry about what they do. If they want internet connections, they can use the computers at school at lunchtime or at break or in homework clubs. They can use the computers in the library too.*
>
> *Foster Mother*

(These guidelines were written from the material of the Stopitnow campaign, and from discussions with the Foster Plus support group in Abingdon and the Foster Carers' support group in Witney).

Finally

Technology moves at an increasingly fast pace and it can sometimes feel like the developments outstrip our capacity to understand and use it. Parents and carers need to learn as much as they can about the use of computers and the internet, if the young people for whom they care, are using the technology in the home. If a parent/carer feels their knowledge and understanding falls short of what is useful, then consulting reputable retailers, or ICT staff in schools/colleges, might be a useful way to seek additional information and advice.

Computers can be used for cyberbullying, see the next section. If the supervision of young people is punitive or has the effect of scaremongering, then the likelihood that they will talk to us as supervising adults is limited. It is important to allow young people to use the technology, while taking a positive role with regard to supervision.

Mobile phones

We held out for quite a while against buying our foster son a mobile phone, despite much pleading. We were worried about potential health risks, how he would use it, and whether he would lose it or have it taken from him. Now he has gone to secondary school, he has to travel on the bus by himself, there are times when he needs to stay later for clubs, and apparently, everyone else has one! So we bought him one at Christmas. He was so pleased that our worries took a back seat for a time. I have recently begun to worry again. This time about how he uses the phone. He always has the phone on him, and if it rings he leaves the room to answer it, and doesn't say who it is. I get the impression that he is worried about something or someone, but he doesn't feel he can tell us. Any ideas?

Foster Dad

It is really difficult when you notice a change in your child but you have no idea why this might be the case. If your foster son has recently moved to secondary school, he will be also approaching adolescence. Adolescence is a time of great change for all children, physically, intellectually, socially and emotionally. Many adolescents strive to separate themselves from their parents. It may be that this is what you are seeing.

It could also be more serious. There may be problems around his use of his mobile phone. Do you know what are the school rules about pupils who have mobile phones? Most schools will say they prefer that the phones are not brought into school. In practice, if pupils keep their phones on silent and in their bags, most teachers won't challenge a pupil about them. Cyberbullying is becoming a big problem in schools and this takes place through mobile phones, as many are smart phones have internet connections. This kind of bullying is very serious, it can include:

- Spreading gossip or untrue information.
- Posting or forwarding private information.
- Threats and abuse.
- Exclusion from online groups.
- Impersonation of the victim.
- Filming bullying and circulating images on line.
- Promoting unhelpful or harmful behaviours such as suicide attempts, self-harm, eating disorders.

Cyber bullying differs from other forms of bullying and it is more likely to be devastating and hard to tackle. This is because:

- It can have an impact of greater scale and scope than other forms of bullying.
- The people involved may be very different from the usual profiles of bullies and their victims.
- Cyberbullying can take place any time 24/7 and any place.
- The person being bullied will not always know who is attacking them.
- Some pupils may not be aware that what they are doing is bullying.
- The target of the bullying will have evidence, if they retain it and share it with an adult who can help.

The advice for parents is that in the first place, the best way to deal with cyberbullying is to prevent it happening. Although it is hard to believe, parents need to be aware that their child may as likely be a cyberbully as the target of cyberbullying. Children can get caught up in it all, without thinking about the consequences of what they are doing. It is very important that you talk to your son about the ways he uses his mobile phone and the internet.

Most mobile phone providers and software/services on the internet have in-built safety features. Find out about these for yourself and talk to him about these.

If it is happening then you need to use established strategies.

- There is an anti cyberbullying code, which includes not replying or retaliating to cyberbullying, as well as not assisting a cyberbully by forwarding messages.

- You should keep the evidence so you can report an incident and help to identify the bully. So keep copies of text messages, voice messages, emails, or online conversations on social network sites.

- Report incidents to the school if the incident involves a pupil(s) at the school. Schools have a legal duty to support pupils being bullied and to apply sanctions to the pupil(s) who are perpetrators of bullying.

- Report incidents to the service providers who have complaints and abuse policies. Most responsible service providers can provide information and advice on how to help your child.

- Consider informing the Police if the cyberbullying is serious. It may be that a potential criminal offence has been commtited, such as harassment, stalking, threats of harm or violence to a person or property, evidence of sexual exploitation such as distributing sexual images, inappropriate sexual contact or behaviour.

The website www.anti-bullyingalliance.org.uk has a parents section with links to recommended organisations who can help with bullying.

11. Exams

As parents/carers, we all have memories of the pressures and anxieties of this time of year. Here are some ideas to help you to help the young people for whom you care.

- **Make sure you know what subjects they are taking exams in, when the exams are, and where they take place.** Make sure they know this too! Having a timetable up on the kitchen notice board or on the fridge, helps everyone to be clear and sets a tone in the house that the family thinks exams are important.

- **If the young person has special educational needs - check whether there are any special 'Access Arrangements' in place for them.** These are special arrangements, which are requested in advance by the Special Educational Needs Co-ordinator, such as extra time, a reader, a scribe, and supervised rest breaks. It will be a great help if you can discuss these with the young person. For example, extra time can be best used in different ways for different subjects:

    o For writing a plan before answering a question, for example for essay based answers.
    o For working more slowly throughout the exam, for example labelling diagrams.
    o For checking over answers at the end, for example checking spelling.

  If you feel they are not sure how best to use the Access Arrangements, encourage them to ask the SENCO.

- **Revision needs to not be a last minute affair.** It is best done in stages:

    o Check that they have all the notes for the subject, exercise books in date order, and/or files with paper notes in order in topic groups.

    o They then need to read through all the notes carefully, checking they understand each topic. If they don't, they need to see the subject teacher and ask for help, or ask when there might be a revision support session in school.

    o They then need to make a summary of the key points, either at the end of the notes on each topic or on cards. Having them on cards can be useful, as they are more portable and can be a last minute revision aid on the day.

- **Learning school work for examinations needs to be planned and organized.** Discuss with the young person how they feel they learn best. There are three ways we all learn, by seeing, hearing and doing. Most of us learn all three ways, but it is common for people to have a preferred way. If that is the case for the young person, discuss with them how they can use their preferred way to help themselves:

    o Seeing - if the young person is a visual learner and can visualise the notes they are learning, a use of colour or diagrams or 'mind maps' can be a help.

    o Hearing - if the young person remembers what is said to them, then repeating revision points out loud over and over or listening to taped recordings of their notes can be a help.

    o Doing - if the young person needs to learn from doing, then learning the work, covering it up and writing it out again, and then checking it against the original, can be a help.

  There are no magic shortcuts, learning stuff for examinations is time consuming!

- **There is much that you can do as a parent/carer.**

    o Ensure that the young person has regular sleep and enough sleep as late nights don't help.

    o Provide regular meals and if you can, help the young person to reduce their intake of junk food, fizzy drinks, and if it's an issue, alcohol.

    o Negotiate with the young person when and where they will revise and provide support for revision sessions, quiet times, a favourite hot drink, biscuits, praise.

    o It is not a good idea to revise for long periods of time, particularly if the young person becomes fed up and tired. Help them to plan to revise for a length of time that they feel is manageable, and build in breaks. An hour is plenty, followed by a break when they can show you what they have done, listen to some music, walk around and relax, before starting again.

    o Hopefully, there will be no upsets for the young person in the weeks before the exam. These might include broken bones, a bereavement, a serious illness. However, if there are and you feel that these will affect the young person, you should let the school know. In some cases an application can be made to an examination board for allowances to be made.

- Examinations are an opportunity for young people to show what they know and get recognition for this. Examination successes can open the way to more study and employment opportunities. Young people need to understand that you want them to do their best, but not to be so anxious that they worry or feel that not doing as well as they hoped is a disaster. There can be retakes for some exams and different opportunities to succeed after school at college or on a training course.

- Ensure on the day of the exam that they get up in enough time, have breakfast, have got their pens/pencils, and their last minute notes to reread.

- It is very important that they get to the examination room 10 minutes before the exam starts. Arriving late and flustered will affect their confidence and performance. Please note that if they are late, they will only be allowed in for a short time after the exam has started, after that they will simply not be allowed in.

- Reassure the young person that you want them to do their best.

- At the end of the day after the exam, ask how it went and listen to them.

If you have specific questions or worries, contact the school straight away. There are staff there who will help, these are: the Form Tutor, the teacher for a particular subject, the Head of Year, the Designated Teacher for Looked After Children, and the Special Educational Needs Co-ordinator.

Social story for preparing for exams

When children and young people are anxious, they can feel overwhelmed. Exams can be overwhelming for them. It is hard for parents/carers to know what to say that will help. Social stories can be helpful when someone is feeling anxious and over whelmed. Social stories are short descriptions of a particular situation, event or activity, which include information about what to expect in that situation and why. Social stories were created by Carol Grey in 1991, to help to teach social skills to people on the Autistic Spectrum. They can be very useful to other people too, and particularly to children. On the next page is a social story for children about preparing for exams. It may be that this is a help to you with regard to what you can say to help your child at this time.

Social Story - Preparing for exams

School is about learning new ideas and skills. Some of the different subjects you study are decided by Government guidelines and some are options you chose.

Sometimes, learning is easy. Other times, it can be hard, especially when the ideas and skills are new. If you find the work hard, **ask for help,** it is the job of your teacher to help you.

Teachers and staff in school can help you by **explaining or demonstrating different ways to understand the work.** They can tell you what you need to do step by step.

Staff can also help by **asking you questions or setting tests for you.** This way they can find out what you do know. Then they will support you to think of answers.

At the end of a course of learning, you will be expected to do an exam.

Sometimes pupils feel nervous **before an exam.** It is okay to feel nervous.

Here are some ideas to help you:

- The teacher will tell you what work will be tested in the exam. **Listen to your teacher, so you know what to revise.**

- **Believe in yourself,** you have done the work over the years in school.

- Think **positive,** stop worrying thoughts, tell yourself 'I can only do my best'.

- **Ask for help if you need it,** don't struggle on your own.

- **Find a good place and have times,** when you can revise at home.

- Take your revision **one step at a time.**

- When you are revising, **have breaks and reward yourself** (chocolate biscuits or your favourite music can help!).

- Have times when you **relax:** listen to music; have a bath; watch a favourite tv programme; play a computer game (but not for too long!!).

- Look after yourself get enough: **sleep, good food, exercise and rest.**

Exclusions

My boy is 13 years old and he goes to our local secondary school. The school is regularly ringing me up and asking me to come and get him, and to take him home because he is disrupting lessons. They describe it as 'cooling down' time, but it is affecting my job, as I then have to have time off to be at home with him. On top of that, I suspect he prefers to be at home. I tell him he can't watch the television and play on his DS, because he has been in trouble in school, but he doesn't seem to mind that.

Foster Carer

This is a difficult situation for you. Well done for showing your support for your boy and for the school. It may be that the school staff feel they are being helpful, but there are very clear regulations about exclusions, which is what this 'cooling down' time is. You haven't mentioned what kinds of disruptive behaviour your boy has presented in school and whether you are aware of the staff trying different strategies to manage him before this decision to exclude him.

Here are some key points of information about exclusions:

- I suggest you ask for a meeting with the Designated Teacher for Looked After Children to discuss the situation. Explain that you think he likes being at home and so this might not be the best way to make a point to him.

- Ask the school to explain what strategies it has tried and check that they are consulting with relevant professionals, such as your boy's Social Worker, Behaviour Support Teachers, the Educational Psychologist.

- There is no legal basis for a school to suggest a 'cooling down' time, if the school has not formally excluded your boy. Even for short periods of time, a part of the school day must be recorded as an exclusion. Informal or unofficial exclusions are illegal, regardless of whether the arrangement is made with the agreement of the parent/carer.

- Only the Headteacher, or a teacher acting as Head-in-charge, can exclude a student.

- All schools have rules and a behaviour policy. If a student breaches the rules and strategies used by staff have been ineffective, then a decision may be taken to exclude the student.

- Usually exclusions are for a fixed period of time and are generally fixed at the shortest time necessary, one to three days are often long enough.

- It may be that a Headteacher takes a decision to permanently exclude a student. It is usual that this very serious step is only taken following a wide range of other strategies being first tried by school staff.

- There will be exceptional circumstances where, in the Headteacher's judgement, a decision is taken to exclude a student for a first time or 'one-off' offence. These might include:
    - Serious actual or threatened violence against another student or member of staff.
    - Sexual abuse or assault.
    - Supplying an illegal drug.
    - Carrying an offensive weapon.

  Then the school will inform agencies involved with the student, as well as the parent/carer, and consider whether to also inform the Police.

- When a school has excluded a student for six days or longer, the school has a duty to arrange full-time educational provision for the student.

- Parents/carers have a duty to ensure that their children, if excluded, are not in public places during normal school hours, regardless of whether the parent/carer is with the child.

12. Glossary

Academies are all ability state-funded independent schools. They are established and managed by sponsors from a wide range of backgrounds: business; universities; other schools; faith or voluntary groups. They are run by an Academy Trust, which employs the staff. They don't have to follow the national curriculum and they can set their own term times. They have to follow the same rules on admissions, special educational needs, and exclusions, as state schools. They are set up with the backing of the Local Authority, but they are not maintained by them. There is close collaboration between the Local Authority and Academies in their area.

Access Arrangements, these are available for all examinations in line with the Disability Discrimination Act 1995. These are pre-examination adjustments, which can be applied for, to give all candidates the opportunity to demonstrate in examinations, their skills, knowledge and understanding of the work they have done. Applications for particular access arrangements are made on the basis of evidence of need. Need can include a disability, special educational needs such as dyslexia, a temporary difficulty such as a broken arm, or psychological problems such as a bereavement. Applications should be applied for as early as possible, with supporting evidence of eligibility provided by a professional whose qualifications are acceptable to the Joint Council for Qualifications. Various arrangements can be requested such as alternative accommodation for the exam, Braille question papers, extra time up to a maximum of 25%, a reader, a scribe, supervised rest breaks, a word processor, etc.

Accommodated, some parents have difficulties promoting the development and well being of their child(ren). If these are referred to Social and Health Care, and after home-based strategies have been tried, children may be accommodated with parental agreement and support, with relatives or friends, in foster care, or in a children's home.

Adoption, the legal transfer of parental responsibility from the birth parents to the adoptive parents. This can only be done by a court. The child is then a permanent member of the adoptive family, the child takes the family's name, and a new birth certificate is issued

Advanced Skills Teacher (AST), a teacher who has been promoted because of their excellent teaching skills, and who advises other teachers, usually in several schools.

Advisory Centre for Education (ACE), a voluntary body which exists to offer information and independent advice about education for parents and carers.

ATTACH Team, is a specialist service working closely with CAMHS in Oxfordshire, offering consultation, direct work and service development work with Looked After and adopted children, and their families.

Behaviour Support Teacher (BST), a specialist teacher who visits schools on a regular basis to support pupils, staff and parents with pupils' emotional and behavioural issues.

Bursary Fund, is money that a young person (16-19 years) or their education or training provider, can use to pay for clothing, books, course equipment, transport and lunch on study and training days. The young person must be studying at school or college (not university) in England. There is a different scheme in Wales, Scotland and Northern Ireland (see Education Maintenance Grant).

CAFCASS - The Children and Family Court Advisory and Support Service, is a dedicated national service to promote the best interests of children involved in family court proceedings.

Care Order, a court order obtained on the basis of evidence that the child's development and well being cannot be promoted without an order. Once an order is granted, the Social Worker has shared parental responsibility.

Care Plan, there is an assessment of a child when she/he enters care. The Social Worker must ensure that the child's needs and the services to meet these needs, are set out in the care plan. A care plan should be drawn up before a child becomes Looked After, or in the case of an emergency entry to care, within 14 days. The care plan includes key documents such as the Health Plan and the Personal Education Plan **(PEP).**

Child and Adolescent Mental Health Service (CAMHS), a team of psychiatrists, clinical psychologists, psychiatric nurses and family therapists, who assess and treat children and young people who may have mental health difficulties/issues.

Child Protection Plan, when there are concerns that a child(ren) is being significantly harmed, Social and Health Care are required by law to investigate these. If there is evidence this is the case, a case conference will be called to discuss concerns with other agencies and decide whether there needs to be a child protection plan.

Children's Guardian, is an independent person appointed by a family court to represent the rights and interests of a child in court proceedings. They are qualified and experienced in social work with children and families. They were previously known as 'Guardians ad litem.'

City technology colleges, are independent schools in urban areas that are free. They have an emphasis on technologicaland practical skills. They are owned and funded by companies as well as by central government, not by the Local Authority.

Code of Practice, has guidance relating to children and young people with a disability as well as those with special educational needs. It covers the age range of 0-25 years. It replaces the Code of Practice 2001, and it reflects the changes introduced by the Children and Families Act 2014. There is a clearer focus on the views of children and young people and parents. It also contains guidance on publishing a local offer of support for children and young people with special educational needs or disabilities. For children with more complex needs, a coordinated assessment process and the new 0-25 Education Health and Care Plan (EHCP) replaces Statements and learning disability assessments (LDAs).

Common Assessment Framework (CAF), is designed to be used as an assessment tool by the whole children's workforce to assess the additional needs of children and young people, at the first sign of difficulties.

Core group, when a child protection plan is made at a Child Protection Initial Case Conference, the conference identifies a smaller (core) group of professionals who will be responsible for implementing the plan. They meet regularly to share information and co-ordinate their work to support the child(ren) and family.

Corporate parent, as the corporate parent of children in care, a Local Authority has a legal and moral duty to provide the kind of loyal support that any good parents would provide for their own children. Corporate parenting emphasises that it is the Local Authority as a whole, not just its Social Work department, which has responsibility for the child.

Cyberbullying, can be defined as the use of Information and Communications Technology (ICT), particularly mobile phones and the internet, deliberately to upset someone else. It can be an extension of face-to-face bullying, with technology providing the bully with another route to harass their target. However, it differs in several significant ways from other kinds of bullying: the invasion of home and personal space, the difficulty in controlling electronically circulated messages, the size of the audience, perceived anonymity, and even the profile of the person doing the bullying and the target.

Designated Teacher, a member of staff in each school who has the responsibility to know the children in public care, arrange support where needed and liaise with the other agencies, especially the Social Worker for the child.

Education Health and Care Plan (EHCP), a statutory document issued by the Local Authority which sets out the special educational needs of a child together with the resources that child needs to make progress in school. The document names the school that is deemed to be an appropriate placement to meet the child's needs. Plans must be reviewed annually.

Education Maintenance Allowance (EMA), provides a financial incentive for young people to stay on in education post 16 years. This is only available to young people in education or training in Wales, Scotland and Northern Ireland (for young people in England, see Bursary Fund).

Educational Psychologist (EP), visits schools, nurseries, and family centres on a regular basis working with teachers, parents and other professionals in a joint problem solving capacity to assist children's learning and behaviour, assess psychological development and special educational needs.

Education Social Worker (ESW), visits schools on a regular basis to monitor attendance, advise staff about keeping attendance registers, and promoting attendance when there are concerns. They work with parents where they have difficulties getting their child(ren) to attend school regularly.

Elective home education is the term used by the Department for Children, Schools and Families to describe the decision made by parents/carers to provide education for their children at home instead of sending them to school. This is different from home tuition provided by a Local Authority or education provided by a Local Authority in a place other than a school. The children are not registered at a school, including mainstream schools, special school, independent schools, academies and Pupil Referral Units.
Parents/carers chose home education for a variety of reasons. The Local Authority's remit is not with regard to the reason for the choice, but with the suitability of the education provided. The responsibility for a child's education rests with its parents/carers. In England, education is compulsory, but school is not. The law states:

> *'The parent (or carer) of every child of compulsory school age shall cause him to receive efficient full-time education suitable to his age, ability and aptitude and to any special educational needs he may have' (Section 7 of the Education Act 1996).*

Each Local Authority provides information about elective home education and has a duty to establish the identities of children in their area not receiving a suitable education. Local Authorities have no statutory duties to monitor the quality of home education on a routine basis.

Emotional and behavioural difficulties (EBD), refers to young people whose emotions and behaviour are presenting significant hindrance to their social and educational success. Sometimes these difficulties are referred to as BESD, behaviour, emotional and social difficulties.

Exclusions, a decision taken by the Headteacher in response to a breach of the school's behaviour policies. Informal or unofficial exclusions are illegal. Fixed period exclusions should be for the shortest time necessary. Permanent exclusions are usually the final step following a range of strategies, which have been tried without success. In exceptional circumstances, a Headteacher may judge it appropriate to exclude for a single offence.

Extended schools, offer a range of services and activities during and outside school hours, to help meet the needs of children and young people, their families, and the wider community. These can include: support for family learning, access to IT equipment and software, breakfast and after-school clubs.

EYSENIT (Early Years SEN Inclusion Teachers) support and advise parents of pre-school children with significant special needs, developing home-based learning programmes with them and other professionals working with pre-school age children.

Faith schools, are associated with a particular religion. They can be different kinds of schools: voluntary aided schools, free schools, and academies. They have to follow the national curriculum, except for religious studies, where they are free to only teach about their own religion. The admissions criteria and staffing policies may be different, although anyone can apply for a place.

Family Support Worker (FSW), are support staff, who work with the guidance of Social Workers to advise children and families.

Foster care, this is provided by single people, parents, families who care for children when their own families (family of origin) are not able to do so. Foster care can be short term, long term, foster plus for children with complex high level needs, or fostering for young people on remand. Foster carers must be approved by fostering services and are registered with the Commission for Social Care Inspection.

Foundation School, is a type of school which has a degree of independence from the Local Authority. The School Governors control admissions to the school, employ the school staff, and own the school's estate.

Free schools, are 'all ability' schools, which can't use academic selection processes. They are funded by the government, they are not run by the Local Authority. They have more control over how they do things. They don't have to follow the national curriculum. They can set their own pay and conditions for staff and they can change the length of school terms and the school day. They are set up by: charities, universities, independent schools, community and faith groups, teachers, parents, and businesses.

General Practitioner (GP), family doctor who advises and treats general illnesses, and refers to more specialist medical services.

Health visitor, a nurse who has had extra training in advising parents on issues such as feeding problems, immunisations, behaviour difficulties, support, and local services.

Independent Panel of Special Education Advisers (IPSEA), gives free advice to parents/carers of children with special educational needs.

Independent School, has the freedom to set its own curriculum and to choose its pupils. They are not dependent on Government and Local Authority finance. Pupils are admitted on a fee paying arrangement.

Individual education plan (IEP), is a way of planning, teaching and reviewing what is arranged in school for children with special educational needs. It is a working document for all teaching staff, recording key short-term targets and strategies for an individual pupil that are different from or additional to those inplace for the rest of the group or class.

Key Stage 1 (KS1), the National Curriculum year groups 1 and 2.

Key Stage 2 (KS2), the National Curriculum year groups 3, 4, 5 and 6.

Key Stage 3 (KS3), the National Curriculum year groups 7, 8 and 9.

Key Stage 4 (KS4), the National Curriculum year groups 10 and 11.

Kinship Care, is an arrangement where a child, who cannot be cared for by their parents, goes to live with a relative or a family friend. It has the advantage of making it easier for a child to keep in touch with family members and friends, which may help them maintain their religion, language and culture. If a private Kinship arrangement is likely to last longer than six weeks, the Local Authority needs to be involved and to assess the suitability of the carer. A Kinship carer may apply to the Court for a Residence Order, a Special Guardianship Order, or an Adoption Order. Alternatively the Kinship carer may ask to be assessed as a long term carer for the child.

Life Story Work, when children are separated from their birth families, they can lose the chance to discuss what happened in the past and to make sense of it all as they grow and develop. Life Story Work is a process of getting more information, sharing memories on the basis of the information with a trusted adult, and the child getting support for things that have happened previously or that are a problem for them currently. Life Story Work provides children with a structured and understandable way of talking about themselves. It is also a basis for adults to listen to children and respect their views.

Local Authority (LA), the Local Authority is responsible for all local government functions in its area, including schools.

Multi-agency, when professionals from more than one agency work together.

National Curriculum, Government national guidelines with regard to what is taught in schools.

National Curriculum Year Groups,

Foundation Stage 3	2-3 years
Foundation Stage 2	3-4 years
Foundation Stage 1	4-5 years

Primary School	Year 1	5-6 years
	Year 2	6-7 years
	Year 3	7-8 years
	Year 4	8-9 years
	Year 5	9-10 years
	Year 6	10-11 years
Secondary School	Year 7	11-12 years
	Year 8	12-13 years
	Year 9	13-14 years
	Year 10	14-15 years
	Year 11	15-16 years
Sixth Form	Year 12	16-17 years
	Year 13	17-18 years

Ofsted - Office for Standards in Education, is the official body for inspecting schools.

P Scales, these are used to measure the progress made by children and young people with learning disabilities aged 5 - 16 who are working below NC level 1. The P scales have 8 levels starting at P1 and progressing to P8.

Pastoral support programme (PSP), is set up to help a pupil who is at serious risk of disaffection or exclusion. If in addition, the pupil has SEN, the IEP should reflect appropriate strategies to meet their needs.

Pathway plan, the Children (Leaving Care) Act 2000 introduced a new duty on local authorities to support Looked After young people beyond the age of 16 years. The plan must set out the services and the practical and emotional support that they require, so that they are able to make a successful transition from living in care to a more independent lifestyle.

Personal Adviser, personal advisers can provide information, advice, guidance and support for young people aged 13 - 19 years, including vulnerable young people requiring more substantial one-to-one support. The key objective is to support young people to remain in learning and to fulfil their potential.

Personal education plan (PEP), some pupils in public care have under performed in school. The PEP is led by the Social Worker and the Designated Teacher in school, and is aimed at ensuring that these pupils achieve as well as possible in school.

Pupil Premium, pupil premium funding is additional funding made to publicly funded schools in England, to raise the attainment of disadvantaged pupils and close the gap between them and their peers. Schools receive £1,900 for each pupil who is: in the Looked After System, adopted, subject to a special guardianship order/ child arrangements order/ a residence order, premiums are also made for children who are eligible for free school meals and children in service families. Schools manage this funding in different ways and report on how the funding has been used an annual basis to their governing body. This report may be on the school website.

Private schools (also known as independent schools), charge fees to attend. They have their own admissions criteria and are selective with regard to the pupils they will admit to the school. They don't have to follow the national curriculum. They are not funded by government, but they must be registered with the government and they are regularly inspected.

'Round Robin', this is an informal way of collecting the opinions of teachers in secondary schools with regard to concerns about an individual child.

Safeguarding, all those in contact and working with children and families have a duty to safeguard and promote children's welfare. Safeguarding involves:
- Protecting children from maltreatment.
- Preventing impairment of children's health and development.
- Ensuring that children are growing up in circumstances consistent with the provision of safe and effective care.
- Taking action to enable all children to have the best chances.

Working Together to Safeguard Children 2015

School nurse, visits school on a regular basis to ensure the health needs of children in school are met, and acts as a link to other health services.

SEN register, is kept in schools and colleges. A child or young person has a learning difficulty if she/he has significantly greater difficulty in learning than the majority of others of the same age or has a disability which prevents or hinders her/him from making use of facilities of a kind generally provided for others of the same age in mainstream schools or mainstream post-16 education settings.

Social stories, are short descriptions of a particular situation, event or activity, which include information about what to expect in that situation and why. Social stories were created by Carol Grey in 1991, to help to teach social skills to people on the Autistic Spectrum. They can be very useful to other people too, and particularly to children.

Social workers, advise families about services available and assess children and families' needs for support including respite care and short-term/long term care.

Special educational needs (SEN), refers to any difficulty a young person may have that affects their educational achievement or behaviour in school. The broad areas of need are:
- Communication and interaction.
- Cognition and learning.
- Social, emotional and mental health difficulties.
- Sensory and/or physical needs.

Special educational needs co-ordinator (SENCO), there is one in every school.

The SENCO has the key responsibilities:

- Overseeing the day-to-day operation of the school's SEN policy.
- Co-ordinating provision for children with SEN.
- Liaising with the relevant Designated Teacher where a looked after. child has SEN.
- Advising on the graduated approach to providing SEN support.
- Advising on the deployment of the school's delegated budget and other resources to meet pupils' needs effectively.
- Liaising with parents of pupils with SEN.
- Liaising with early year's providers, other schools, educational psychologists, health and social care professionals, and independent or voluntary bodies.
- Being a key point of contact with external agencies, especially the local authority and its support services.
- Liaising with potential next providers of education to ensure a pupil and their parents are informed about options and a smooth transition is planned.
- Working with the Head teacher and school governors to ensure that the school meets its responsibilities under the Equality Act (2010) with regard to reasonable adjustments and access arrangements.
- Ensuring schools keep records of all pupils with SEN, up to date.

Special Guardianship, gives carers such as grandparents or existing foster parents, clear responsibility for all aspects of caring for a child or young person, and for taking decisions to do with their upbringing. Special Guardianship preserves the legal link between the child or young person and their birth family, and is accompanied by proper access to a full range of support services.

Standard Attainment Tests (SATS), as from September 2015, the system of levels for children's attainments and progress changed. The change is to allow teachers greater flexibility in the way they plan and assess pupils' learning. The new National Curriculum places far greater emphasis on ensuring that children not only learn new skills and acquire knowledge, but they must also be able to apply them within a range of contexts. Schools are free to choose their own assessment system. Most schools are using systems which reflect the learning steps a child will make before moving from one level to another within a curriculum year. These steps of achievement are:

- Significantly below the expected stage of achievement for their year group (emerging).
- Below the expected stage of achievement for their age group (developing).
- At the expected stage of achievement for their age group (expected).
- Above the expected stage of achievement for their age group
- (mastery).

Key stage SATs are now reported as a scaled score, with a score of 100 representing the expected level for each age group. The national tests are designed to be as similar as possible every year in terms of the demands they place on the children sitting the tests. Using a scaled score makes it possible to compare scores on different tests. The new scaled score of 100 represents the 'national standard'.

State boarding schools, provide free education but charge fees for boarding. They give priority to children who have a particular need to board. They assess the needs of a child's suitability for boarding. Some are run by Local Authorities, and some are run as academies or free schools.

Studio schools, are usually small schools (catering for about 300 pupils) which deliver mainstream qualifications through project based learning. This means working in realistic situations, as well as learning academic subjects. Pupils work with local employers and a personal coach, to follow a curriculum designed to give them the skills and qualifications they will need in work or further education.

Tribunal (SENDIST) Special Educational Needs and Disability Tribunal, a body to whom parents/carers of children, who have special educational needs, can appeal against decisions made by Local Authorities in England, with regard to the education of individual children.

UASC - Unaccompanied Asylum Seeking Children, are children under 18 years who are seeking asylum, having arrived in the country without a parent or guardian. Many will enter the Looked After System.

University technical colleges, specialise in subjects like engineering and construction. They teach these subjects alongside business skills and IT. Pupils study academic subjects as well as practical subjects. The curriculum is designed by the university and employers, who also provide work experience for the pupils. They are sponsored by universities, employers and further education colleges.

Voluntary accommodation, is a term used to cover children who are in the care of the Local Authority under a voluntary agreement, children who are not subject to a Care Order and for whom parental responsibility remains with the parents. Accommodation agreements can be terminated by parents at any time.

Young, Gifted and Talented Programme (YG&T), is a national programme, funded and supported by the Department for Children, Schools and Families (DCSF). It is dedicated to providing opportunities within and outside the classroom for gifted and talented children (4-19 years). Gifted and talented can include a wide range: maths, writing poetry, sport, leadership, creative ideas, etc. Schools and colleges are responsible for deciding who is gifted and talented, according to national and local guidance. They typically identify approximately 10% of their pupils.

Youth Offending Team (YOT), a multi-agency team which works with young people who are at risk of offending, or who have offended.